MEASURE AND MANAGE STRESS

Herbert S. Kindler, Ph.D.
Marilyn Ginsburg, M.A., M.F.C.C.

ELR

12/00

3-30

OCT 31 1995

Crisp Publications
Menlo Park, C

MEASURE AND MANAGE STRESS

Herbert S. Kindler, Ph.D.
Marilyn Ginsburg, M.A., M.F.C.C.

CREDITS
Editor: **Chris Carrigan**
Managing Editor: **Kathleen Barcos**
Typesetter: **Execustaff**
Cover Design: **David Barcos**

Library of Congress Card Catalog Number 93-074715
Kindler, Herbert S.
Ginsburg, Marilyn
Measure and Manage Stress
1-56052-288-7

INTRODUCTION

We wrote this book to help you extend and enrich your life. Over the years, people who participated in our stress management workshops started coming back. They told their success stories of renewed vitality, looking trim and feeling more in charge of their lives.

After more than fifteen years of intensive study, formal research and hundreds of interactive workshops with thousands of participants, we decided to make our program more widely available through this "workshop in print."

We have gained an understanding of what creates stress, how it affects people's lives and what can be done about it. We want you to understand the causes of stress, its consequences and the methods that will allow you to manage your stress effectively.

Our approach is to present a complex subject in a straightforward, practical form you can take into your life and use on a daily basis. It has been helpful to people with widely diverse careers, educational backgrounds and lifestyles. Each chapter contains the *essence* of our material and experience.

This book is written not only to be read, but to be used as a hands-on experience. It is designed to be defaced. Read with pencil in hand, and circle items that might become part of your personal action plan.

We live in a time when the information age relentlessly paces our lives, extended family support is generally missing, and ecological crises and war threaten survival. We have no choice about whether we want to manage stress—we must, or it will manage us.

Pressure is particularly keen in high-performance, high-visibility professions and positions. When we take on responsibility for employees and dependents, we add additional pressure to our lives.

The job of staying healthy and aware is tough, and it is *never* going to be easy. Moreover, the one person you absolutely cannot afford to abuse or lose is *you*.

Our intention is to give you the insights and tools that will enhance the quality of your life during these increasingly stressful times.

CONTENTS

ACKNOWLEDGMENTS

We deeply appreciate the following teachers who personally touched and helped change our lives:

A. H. Almaas, Roberto Assagioli, Mary Burmeister, Sam Culbert, Gene Gendlin, Brugh Joy, Linda Olsen, Lord Pentland, Fritz Perls, Dick Price, David Shapiro, Harry Sloan, Edith Stauffer, Hal Stone, Bob Tannenbaum and Iona Teeguarden

Dedication

To the many clients and workshop participants who opened their hearts to us and gave us valuable feedback, we dedicate these fruits of our mutual learning.

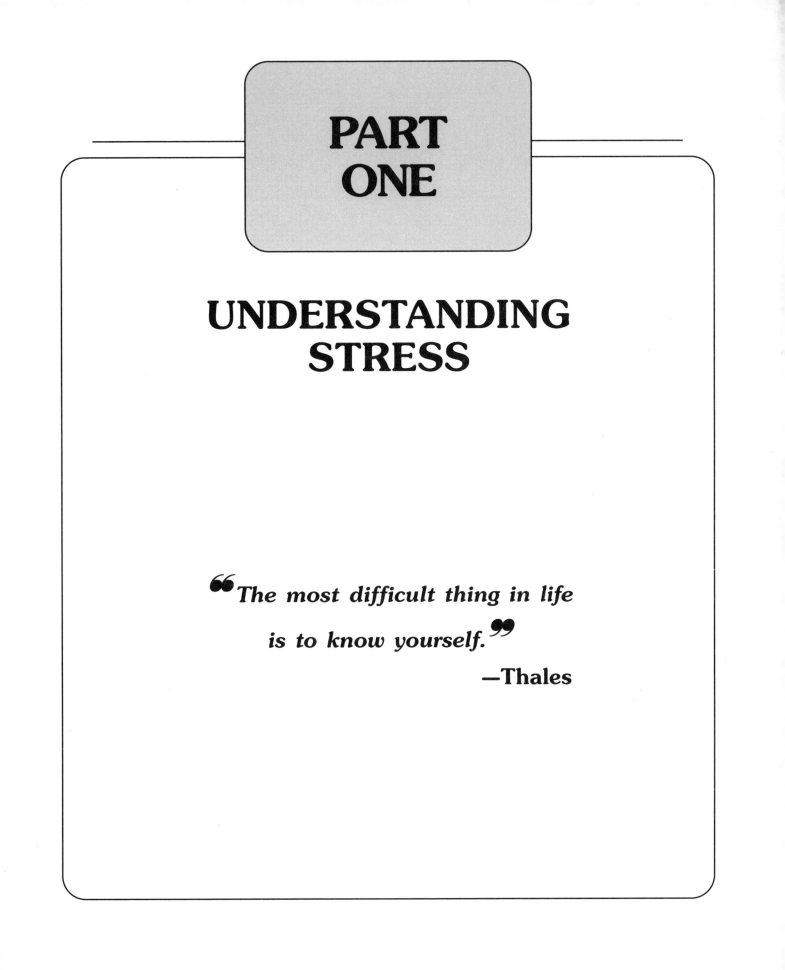

PART ONE

UNDERSTANDING STRESS

"The most difficult thing in life is to know yourself."

—Thales

CHAPTER 1

HOW YOU CAN BENEFIT FROM THIS PROGRAM

Stress is not something you can take or leave. Stress affects your work and personal relationships, even your sex life. It's about life and death.

This stress management program will help you make life choices that release energy for peak performance and heightened personal satisfaction.

Performance and satisfaction benefits rest on these *assumptions* and *guiding principles:*

- You, the reader, are the most qualified person to design your own stress management program. You know what will work for you and what you are willing to work for.

- Renewal involves making conscious choices. You must be willing to confront patterns of behavior that are triggered automatically so that in time your responses become the result of aware decisions.

- The willingness to make a change. Unless you are willing to commit yourself to making positive changes, all the stress management books in the world will not help.

- The essence of stress management is balance. Crucial to your program is finding balance between work and play, relating and having time alone, change and stability, activity and rest, seriousness and lightness, doing and being.

- Your body is the ultimate arbiter of how well your stress management program is serving you. A subtle ongoing communication takes place between your body, feelings and thoughts. Learning how to pay attention and when to act on body messages is essential. These messages may take the form of rashes, allergies, colds or big attention-getters such as a heart attack.

If you agree with the program's assumptions and guiding principles and follow through with your personal action plan, you can expect to reap these *benefits*:

▶ **Improved Performance**

When stress is *very low*, your performance is also low. You have the get-up-and-go of a damp rag. When your stress level is *very high*, performance again suffers—you feel high-strung, like a rubber band stretched to its limit.

Somewhere between these limp and taut extremes is your *peak performance zone*, the middle area in which you do your best work.

Stress and Performance

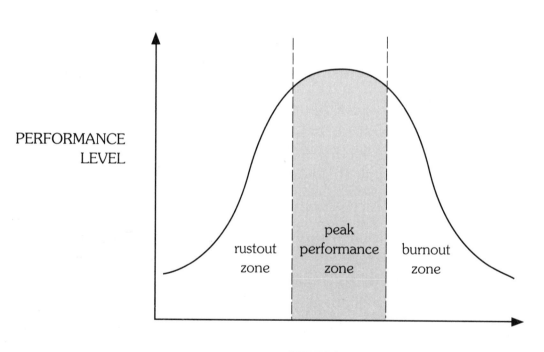

PERFORMANCE LEVEL

rustout zone

peak performance zone

burnout zone

STRESS LEVEL

▶ **Improved Health**

In a study of 1,540 executives, researchers found that managers in both high-stress and low-stress ranges had more medical problems than those in the middle range.[1] Other research shows that individuals suffering prolonged stress had fewer natural "killer cells"—the immune system's most potent defense against harmful micro-organisms.[2]

The major culprit undermining health in urban societies is *relentless pressure.* Stress-related illnesses typically start with annoying physical or emotional symptoms such as:

- headaches
- indigestion
- teeth grinding
- back pain
- irregular menstrual cycles

- mood swings
- irritability
- apathy
- compulsive eating
- hyperactivity

Attention to early signals and the application of appropriate stress management techniques can arrest the development of serious degenerative diseases such as stroke, heart disease, ulcers, rheumatoid arthritis, asthma, diabetes and colitis.

► **Enhanced Relationships**
It is difficult to maintain a satisfying connection with others—either at work or home—when you feel tense. Relationship partners who are suffering from excessive stress are unable to sensitively assert their needs and cannot empathetically attune themselves to others' needs. Effective stress management helps overcome irritability and mood swings.

Individuals who want to learn about stress management are busy. They are reluctant to give up the little free time they have. This resistance was colorfully expressed by one woman, who said: "I can't picture myself sitting like a pretzel, studying my navel while I have a hundred errands to run. Furthermore, I'm definitely not going to give up the few real pleasures left in life—like ice cream and pizza—for wheat germ and radishes!"

As the architect of your own personal stress management program, you can make your life work better without having to "twist yourself into a pretzel."

CHAPTER 2

GETTING A HANDLE ON STRESS

Why is one person's adventure—traveling abroad, facing a new job challenge, falling in love—another's stress?

Stress is how people react to situations that feel taxing. What motivates one person may burden another; what satisfies the boss may annoy her employee. Stress is subjective.

Your Sources of Stress

To explore what feels personally stressful to you at this time, complete the following brief exercises.

Exercise 1

In the column below, list sources of stress that you have experienced during the past two weeks, six sources at home and six sources at work. Stop reading and write your 12 stress sources now.

Sources of Stress at Home   **Sources of Stress at Work**

1._____   1._____

2._____   2._____

3._____   3._____

4._____   4._____

5._____   5._____

6._____   6._____

Below are a few sources of stress that others have experienced:

- "I realize my boss doesn't know what he's doing."

- "My wife is menopausal and our sex life is depressing."

- "My top salesperson quit and went to work for our toughest competitor."

- "After I pulled together a terrific team, we lost a big client. Now I have to decide whom to lay off."

- "I got rear-ended by an uninsured driver."

- "The dishwasher overflowed and ruined our new carpet."

- "I just learned that my boss is having an affair with my secretary."

These diverse examples have one common thread: Every stress source on the list is *external* to the individual. However, external sources are merely the visible tip of the stress management iceberg. *Internal* or self-generated stress, which is hidden from view, is more difficult to identify.

Exercise 2

Think back over the past two weeks. What are some ways in which you created pressure or anxiety for *yourself?*

_____

_____

_____

_____

_____

_____

_____

_____

_____

_____

If you have difficulty coming up with self-generated stress sources, review the examples below. If they stimulate additional ideas for your list, add them.

- "I'm a *perfectionist*. Nothing is ever quite good enough."

- "I'm a *worrier*. I can't leave my work at the office, and I keep rehashing what I wish I had said."

- "I'm a *workaholic*. I feel overloaded but I still do extra work."

- "I hate to admit it, but I'm a *procrastinator*."

- "I'm *super-responsible*. I only delegate to people I trust will be as diligent as I in handling a task. (I keep looking, but never seem to find such a person.)"

- "I'm so *self-critical* that I become paralyzed and tongue-tied."

- "I'm a *people-pleaser*. I have trouble saying no and I overcommit my time."

Stress is your response to events, both external and self-generated, that tax your abilities and resources beyond your ability to cope. Almost invariably, we react to a stress stimulus with a visceral reflex. If a small child chasing a ball suddenly darts in front of your speeding car, your instinctive physiological reflex will occur.

Most contemporary situations that provoke stress do not involve physical danger; they involve angry coworkers, dented fenders, feelings of inadequacy, impatient customers, burnt toast and canceled car insurance. In these types of situations, we usually have the option of reappraising the stress trigger and responding with awareness. Most often, we have no need for an immediate response and can reframe the stress stimulus as a problem to be solved.

With the power of conscious perception, you can create a crucial gap—a space between the stimulus and the response—where it is at least possible to have some degree of choice. The cornerstone of stress management is the knowledge that gaining control over our lives depends not so much on what is happening, but on *how we choose to react*.

As you become more aware of your unconscious patterns, you will have access to a broader range of creative possibilities. "Freedom," suggests Rollo May, "is the individual's capacity to pause between stimulus and response, and throw his weight on the side of one particular response among many."

Review

> ### *Your Personal Action Options*
> ### BECOMING AWARE OF STRESS
>
> **1. External Sources**
>   Recognize stress from your work, others and your environment.
>
> **2. Internal Sources**
>   Ask yourself: "In what ways am I contributing to my own stress?"

CHAPTER 3

THE BIG PICTURE:
USING A CYBERNETICS SYSTEMS MAP

With the help of a cybernetic systems model, you will learn how to manage stress effectively by connecting with your personal vision.

Gaining *conscious perception* through our cybernetic system is the beginning of bringing the stress response under your control. It is the most powerful tool you can use to create a context in which stress-evoking events become readily manageable.

Cybernetic comes from the Greek word for "to steer."[1] With a personal vision, you can steer a safe and satisfying course through life. Without a vision, you drift. The combination of an inspiring vision and a systems map helps you maintain your life direction while reducing excess stress. Follow the map on the next page as we describe each of its parts.

Personal Vision

Clarity of vision reduces stress in your life. In articulating one or more visions for this period in your life, let yourself stretch beyond where you are: Dare to dream. Dreams do not materialize automatically. Through envisioning, they become possibilities. Oscar Hammerstein asks rhetorically in *South Pacific*, "If you don't have a dream, how you gonna have a dream come true?"

Cybernetic Systems Map for Stress Management

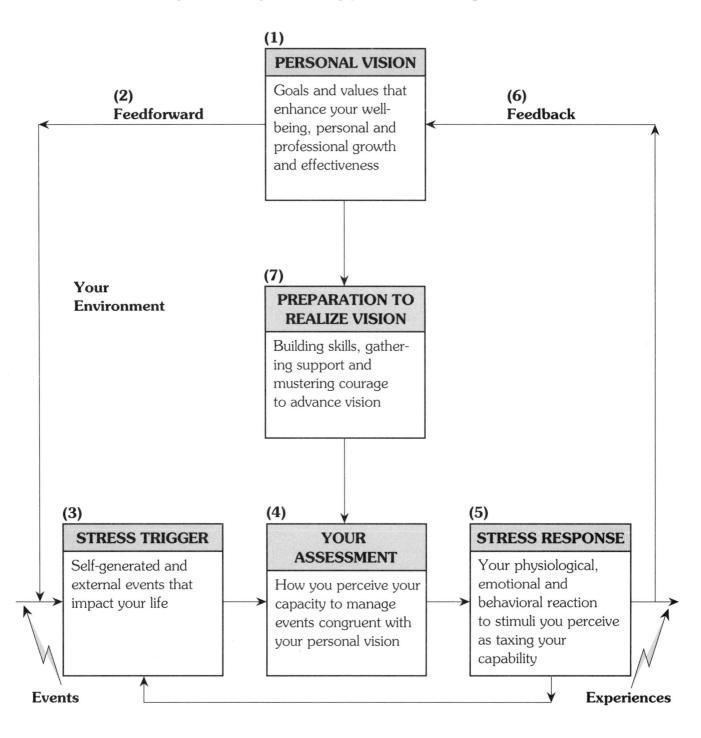

Finding Your Vision

The alchemy of fantasy starts when you envision what you want to be, have and do.

Benefits of having a clear personal vision:

- You can more easily sort through competing claims for your attention.
- Obstacles look less like mountains.
- You attract like-minded people who can join with you.
- Your energy remains focused.

Take all the time you need to complete the following exercise.

Exercise 3

Jot down your first response to the following questions. (Give your imagination free rein.)

1. If you could have three wishes granted, what would they be?

a. _____

_____

b. _____

_____

c. _____

_____

_____

2. If you have only five years to live with no financial limitations, what would you want to do with your life?

_____

_____

_____

_____

_____

_____

3. Name the three people, past or present, you most admire. List the reasons you admire them.

Name	*Reasons*
a. _____	_____
	_____
	_____
b. _____	_____
	_____
	_____
	_____
c. _____	_____
	_____
	_____

4. What are the common threads that connect these people and attract you to them?

_____

_____

_____

_____

_____

_____

_____

5. If you could make just three contributions to the world, what would they be?

a. _____

_____

b. _____

_____

c. _____

_____

6. Find a quiet place where you can unplug the telephone, sit comfortably and take a few deep breaths. Exhale slowly. With each slow exhalation, count down from ten to one, noticing that you become more relaxed with each count. As you feel the day's tension leave your body, reflect on what you have written. Allow time for a clear mental image to form. Picture yourself healthy, radiant and enjoying life fully. Focus softly on your vision until it becomes clear; then, allow it to gently unfold.

Write your vision here. Include the details of each image, thought and feeling. In addition to writing, you may find that making a drawing or rough sketch of your vision is helpful.

In time, your dreams will manifest, energizing every aspect of your life.

Feedforward

To move your dreams from possibility to reality, communicate your aspirations and values to others. These messages are powerful in attracting people with shared interests who may join you to pursue a common vision. Expressing your vision also lets your current contacts know how they can be helpful. The clearer your signal, the more effective it will be in enlisting the support to realize your vision.

A clear picture of what you deeply want and value is positively magnetic, attracting people and resources into your life. A dramatic example is Martin Luther King, who gathered national support with his 1963 "I have a dream" speech.

Stress Trigger

A stress trigger, or source, is any event or impulse that has the potential to elicit a stress response. Triggers are:

► **Outer Events**
A demanding boss, an insensitive co-worker, heavy traffic, a bounced check, smog, family fights.

► **Inner Impulses**
The re-stimulation of past traumas, and the activation of self-protective roles, including the inner "Perfectionist," "Pusher," "Critic," "Worrier" or "Pleaser."

Assessment

Stress is largely an *inside job*. It is your interpretation of a trigger that determines your stress reaction. When a stranger brushes against you, for example, the irritation you feel melts the moment you see him carrying a white cane.

Without conscious perception, a harmless stimulus can automatically trigger a stress response. Assessment is the intervening process in which you give meaning to outer events and inner dialogue. When you assign new meanings, you influence your stress response.

Beliefs, attitudes and values formed in the past filter perceptions. When someone pushes one of your *stress buttons,* they may stimulate a highly charged event from your past. Or, perhaps, the other person may be exhibiting behavior you dislike in yourself.

Your personal vision gives you the power to alter your perception. Events that might otherwise evoke stress become a challenge when seen as possibilities to advance your vision. They are less disturbing when assessed as a chance to stretch or a lesson to be learned. An enclosure for example, may be an overwhelming space, an imprisoning cage, a snug refuge—it all depends on how you perceive and assess it.

Stress Response

Your body reacts to recurring stress by sending you messages—a headache, indigestion, a rash—to capture your attention. The message says: "Help. Something is not working properly. Notice what's going on." The automatic reaction is to stop the annoyance by applying a quick-fix, "Band-Aid" type remedy. Chronic, continuing messages are asking for deeper examination. Until you identify the source of the problem, stress messages recur or escalate.

You can assess the stress triggers in your life as opportunities. When you consciously read early warning signals and begin managing stress with awareness, you empower yourself.

Feedback

Your own stress response to each trigger is valuable feedback. Observe it. (Chapter 4 describes the stress response in detail.)

- Notice if your reaction is appropriate to the triggering source. Most initial stress reactions are automatic. Consciously choose your response as each new circumstance arises.

- Compare what is actually going on in your life with your hopes and dreams. Just as a basketball coach calls "time out" to reassess how well the game plan is working, take time *every day* to ask yourself: "What are my stress reactions trying to tell me?" Your body's signals are a great gift. They give you clues you can use to improve your health.

Through feedback—comparing each stressful experience with your personal vision—you open the possibility of enlarging your self-concept.

Preparation to Realize Your Vision

On the path to attaining your vision, life's inevitable difficulties will be much less unsettling as you increase your competence. The road to mastery demands patience, practice, focus and deferred gratification. The ancient wisdom of the *I Ching* advises, "Perseverance brings good fortune."

Summary: An Example

An inspiring illustration of how the cybernetic systems model works is the story of Shinichi Suzuki, whose vision was realized through teaching 200,000 children to play the violin over a period of 30 years.[2]

▶ **Personal Vision**

Suzuki's *vision* was that all children could learn to play the violin with great proficiency when taught creatively and with love. With amazing patience, he taught four- and five-year-olds to play Bach, Mozart and Vivaldi on tiny instruments.

▶ **Feedforward**

As the *story of his success spread*, large numbers of students enrolled in Suzuki's music program.

▶ **Stress Trigger**

One day, he was challenged by the *desperate plea* of two parents who wanted their blind son to learn to play the violin, which could become a ray of light in the boy's darkness.

▶ **Assessment**

Suzuki *saw no way* in which he could be helpful to the boy or his parents.

► Stress Response

Suzuki experienced *great sadness* and felt a *heaviness* in his chest.

At this point, Suzuki could have suffered his disappointment and not have grown from the experience. This is a common phenomenon when, instead of using a cybernetic systems map, people focus on the sequence shown below.

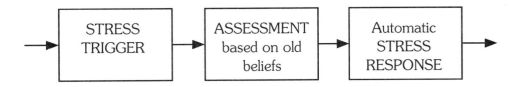

Notice that this sequence provides no learning or personal growth because it is a closed system. When a stimulus is perceived, an automatic response follows. For a different and hopefully less stressful response to occur, the old pattern must be interrupted. You can break your automatic pattern through conscious feedback. Compare your stressful experience with your vision. This feedback opens the possibility of creating a new reality. You open yourself to acquiring new mastery and new perception. In other words, when you relate through feedback to your vision, you are open to gaining mastery and a new perception.

► Feedback to Personal Vision

Suzuki *realized how distressing* this incident was for him, and how it *failed to advance his vision* that all children can learn to play the violin. Rather than abandon the blind child, he developed a plan.

► Preparation to Realize Vision

Suzuki *examined* different teaching methods he might use.

► New Assessment

In his spare time, Suzuki played with his eyes closed until a *shift occurred in his assessment* of the problem. He understood exactly how to proceed with the lessons.

► **New Response**

He invited the boy to embark with him on the joint teaching-learning experiment. Week after week he taught the sightless boy to reach out and precisely touch the tip of his bow in one movement. When he could succeed five times in a row without a miss, *Suzuki's sadness turned to joy.* Not only was the boy eventually able to play the violin; he had real talent.

► **Feedback**

Encouraging feedback mounted over the coming years. The blind student progressed to the concert stage in Tokyo, where he often moved audiences to tears.

Review

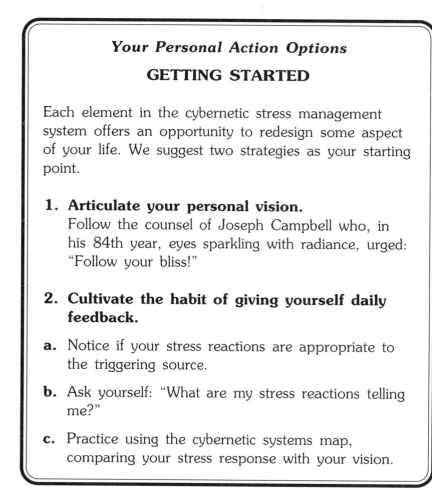

Your Personal Action Options

GETTING STARTED

Each element in the cybernetic stress management system offers an opportunity to redesign some aspect of your life. We suggest two strategies as your starting point.

1. **Articulate your personal vision.**
   Follow the counsel of Joseph Campbell who, in his 84th year, eyes sparkling with radiance, urged: "Follow your bliss!"

2. **Cultivate the habit of giving yourself daily feedback.**

   a. Notice if your stress reactions are appropriate to the triggering source.

   b. Ask yourself: "What are my stress reactions telling me?"

   c. Practice using the cybernetic systems map, comparing your stress response with your vision.

CHAPTER 4

EARLY WARNING SIGNALS
OF STRESS

Stress Signals

Your stress response takes three interconnected forms:

1. Physiological/physical

2. Psychological/emotional

3. Behavioral/action or inaction

Think of a recent graduate, eager to get hired but with serious doubts about making a good enough impression during the job interview. After a restless night and persistent headache, the job applicant experiences all three forms of stress arousal:

▶ **Physiological**
Perspiration, rapid shallow breathing, dry mouth, trembling knees (Tests would have revealed an increase in heart rate and elevated cholesterol.)

▶ **Psychological**
Apprehension, fear of rejection, anxiety, self-doubt

▶ **Behavioral**
Spills coffee on the manager's carpet, bumps into an open door—and, on his way home, devours a huge hot fudge sundae

Of these three reactions, which would you guess is the most reliable indicator of stress?

If you said physiological, you are right. Psychological and behavioral stress reactions vary widely and are less predictable. Some people respond to upset with anger, others with anxiety; some counterattack and others slam doors and withdraw.

Body signals are triggered instinctively. Unless you consciously intervene, they occur automatically, outside your control. As you become sensitive to your body's stress signals, they will offer you dependable, instant feedback that enables you to decide if action is appropriate.

To gain a better understanding of your body's reactions, try the following exercise in a safe, private setting where you will not be disturbed. First read through the instructions; then close your eyes and begin.

Exercise 4

With your eyes closed, go back in time to a recent event that triggered a strong emotional reaction, and *be there*. With this experience clearly in mind, allow your reactions to unfold as they did when the event first occurred.

- If others are involved, look into their faces and observe their expressions. Notice the clothes they are wearing.

- If the event is taking place indoors, carefully observe the room and its furnishings. What colors do you see?

- What is the time? Is it day or night? If daytime, are you warmed by the sun, or is the air cold?

- If nighttime, are clouds or stars overhead?

- What sounds do you hear? Are there traffic noises, music, voices, any unusual odors?

- As this scene becomes increasingly real to you, notice how your body responds.

Your physical reactions play a central role in your stress response. Indicate below what changes you experience in your body during this exercise.

_____

_____

_____

_____

_____

Many people notice one or more of the following stress signals:

- Face becoming flushed
- Heart pounding
- Shortening of breath
- Stomach knotting
- Jaws tightening

- Mouth and throat becoming dry
- Clenching of fists
- Urgency to urinate
- Increased coldness of hands and feet

Our language has incorporated these universal signals. Scary movies are *chillers,* difficult people are *hard to stomach,* and people get *cold feet* in risky situations.

Use the male or female figure on the following page to create a personal stress map by indicating the particular locations where you sense changes occurring in your body. Shade appropriate areas red to show acute symptoms, and blue for chronic pain or illness. Write descriptive words to indicate any physical sensations you are experiencing. Note any connections between illness and your stress symptoms.

Fight or Flight

Throughout the history of human evolution, stress has served a vital survival function. When cave dwellers felt the presence of a roving animal, their stress response prepared them to take appropriate action: fight or flight.

In reaction to the ominous shadow of a saber-toothed tiger on their cave wall, our ancestors instinctively mobilized for action. When dealing with today's *paper tigers,* your stress reflex reactions operate exactly as they did 30,000 years ago, as if your life were actually being threatened.

Our earliest forebears were frequently threatened by physical danger. An immediate stress response was vital to their survival, preparing them to act quickly. As they moved, they dissipated stress. Fighting for your life or running away is not appropriate in everyday office or home situations. Yet, our bodies still equate an angry quarrel with physical danger, and stifling or ignoring those feelings causes a stress buildup that, over time, undermines health.

Locating Stress In Your Body

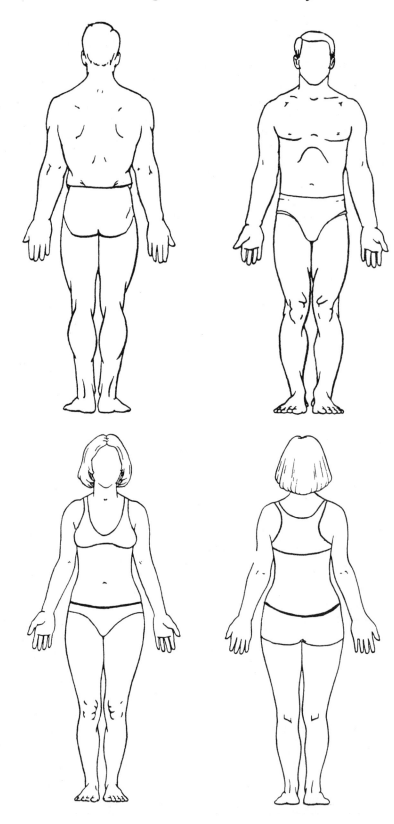

Recognizing Stress Signals

When you feel threatened, an internal fire-alarm sounds, sending your body into full alert. The hypothalamus, a bundle of nerve cells at the very center of your brain, summons your "stress team" to work. The autonomic nervous system speeds the heart rate, stops digestion and activates perspiration; the pituitary gland dispatches hormones into the blood stream.

You can use the summary of the body signals below to monitor stress—your own and others.' Can you relate your physical responses to the self-protective functions described?

Common Body Stress Signals

	Body Signals	Protective Function	Physiological Activity
1	RAPID BREATHING FLUSHED FACE	Faster decision making	More air intake increases the brain's oxygen supply. Blood carries the fresh oxygen to the brain.
2	ENERGY RUSH POUNDING HEART	Energy is mobilized	Adrenaline stimulates the liver to provide more blood sugar. Increased blood circulation delivers energy to muscles.
3	TENSED MUSCLES CHILLED HANDS	Defenses are activated	Muscles are readied to spring into action. Blood supply to the hands is constricted to reduce potential bleeding.
4	DRY THROAT STOMACH CRAMPS	Digestion is stopped	Saliva flow is cut off to conserve digestive energy. Energy is made available for higher-priority needs.

Physical Stress-Response Functions

▶ **Your capacity to make fast decisions expands.** All sensory pathways open wider to collect vital information. Faster breathing brings more oxygen to your brain to speed mental data processing. Peripheral vision blurs, focusing full attention straight ahead on the threat. You hear more, smell more and focus more.

▶ **Your energy level surges.** Breathing speeds and nostrils flare, allowing easier air flow. Increased heart rate circulates oxygen-rich blood. Adrenal glands are stimulated and norepinephrine elevates the heartbeat. Fats, including cholesterol, released into the bloodstream support vigorous muscle activity. The liver produces more glucose, and thyroxine increases the body's metabolism.

▶ **Your defense systems are activated.** Potential bleeding slows as blood vessels just under the skin close in case you are attacked and cut. Morphine-like substances block the perception of pain. To speed clotting, the spleen releases red corpuscles. Muscles tense to prepare the body for aggressive or defensive action.

▶ **Your digestive system is deactivated.** To conserve energy for more vital emergency needs, blood shifts away from stomach and intestines. Sphincter control diminishes and the flow of saliva stops, causing looser bowels and dry mouth.

An important step in your stress management program is being able to witness your body's stress-response signals. Once you are able to observe your instinctual fight-or-flight reaction to stress triggers, you can intervene with a creative response. The Stress Awareness Log is a helpful tool in this process. Here is a sample of one person's log.

STRESS AWARENESS LOG

Name: _____ **Date:** _____

Time	Stress Trigger	Stress Response
7:30 a.m.	My alarm clock didn't go off. I forgot to set it. I need to be on time for 8:00 a.m. meeting.	***Physiological:*** I woke late, my heart pounding. ***Psychological:*** Angry at myself. ***Behavioral:*** I stepped on a wet towel and fell.
8:00 a.m.	I realize that there's no way I'm going to be on time.	***Physiological:*** Headache and upset stomach. ***Psychological:*** I was a bundle of nerves. Feel guilty about being late again. ***Behavioral:*** I gulped my breakfast.
8:30 a.m.	I was half an hour late. My boss said: "Glad you finally decided to join us." Everyone stared at me.	***Physiological:*** My throat was dry. I had heartburn. ***Psychological:*** Embarrassed. It's the third time I've been late in two weeks. Felt like an idiot. ***Behavioral:*** Spilled my coffee.

Exercise 5

During the coming week, choose a day at random to work on your Stress Awareness Log. Every half-hour during that day, record events that trigger your stress response. Then connect each stress trigger, or stimulus, with your body signals, emotional reactions and behavior, to consciously design appropriate intervention strategies. Use the following form to complete this exercise.

STRESS AWARENESS LOG

Day/Date: _____

Time	Stress Trigger	Stress Response
_____	_____	_____
_____	_____	_____
_____	_____	_____
_____	_____	_____
_____	_____	_____
_____	_____	_____
_____	_____	_____
_____	_____	_____
_____	_____	_____
_____	_____	_____
_____	_____	_____
_____	_____	_____
_____	_____	_____
_____	_____	_____
_____	_____	_____
_____	_____	_____
_____	_____	_____

Most people are able to connect their body reactions and their behavior with the source of their stress. Some people have difficulty getting in touch with their feelings. Emotions that are not acknowledged, in time express themselves through the body, attacking points of vulnerability.

Three basic feelings are commonly associated with excessive stress: *anger, sadness* and *fear*. If you have difficulty identifying these three typical responses, here's an approach to help these emotions surface.

► **Anger**

If something prevents you from realizing your goal and you don't experience some tinge of *anger or frustration,* ask yourself, "Where did it go?" Are you eating it? Or is it eating you?

► **Sadness**

Most people experience *sadness* when they lose someone or something they value. If you don't, you may have unexplained irritability or depression later on. Feelings of sadness or tears are appropriate responses to loss.

► **Fear**

Because *fear* implies vulnerability, it is one of the least expressed emotions, and may be covered up with stoicism, false bravado, dependent clinging or withdrawal. Notice how feelings of fear manifest in your body and behaviors.

Exercise 6

After you have completed your Stress Awareness Log, take time out to reflect on what you have written.

1. What triggers do I recognize as recurring sources of unwanted stress?

_____

_____

_____

_____

_____

2. In each case, what in particular led to the *triggering* event?

_____

_____

_____

_____

_____

3. What feelings surfaced in reaction to the trigger? Your *feelings* are a particularly important part of this reflection process; they assist you in uncovering outworn attitudes and beliefs that are inconsistent with your vision, values or present goals.

_____

_____

_____

_____

_____

4. What am I doing to advance my goals and values? Do I engage in behaviors that no longer work for me?

_____

_____

_____

_____

_____

5. What new behaviors or actions would I prefer to express if a similar event occurred?

_____

_____

_____

_____

_____

Using this reflection exercise, the employee with the recurring pattern of getting to work late might realize that something about her current assignment is bothering her. Her action plan might include, in addition to getting to bed earlier, a meeting with her boss to discuss career aspirations and future opportunities.

Review

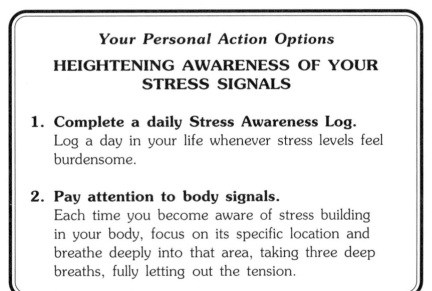

Your Personal Action Options

HEIGHTENING AWARENESS OF YOUR STRESS SIGNALS

1. **Complete a daily Stress Awareness Log.**
   Log a day in your life whenever stress levels feel burdensome.

2. **Pay attention to body signals.**
   Each time you become aware of stress building in your body, focus on its specific location and breathe deeply into that area, taking three deep breaths, fully letting out the tension.

PART TWO

MEASURING
YOUR STRESS

"We need to measure stress to combat disease."

—Hans Selye

CHAPTER 5

THE STRESS TEST

How to resolve troublesome situations without generating more stress is a common challenge. The following story illustrates three approaches to managing life's problems.

> *On the outskirts of a river town, a half-drowned person was seen thrashing about or floating down the river every day for the past month. As each victim was spotted, one of the townspeople dove in and dragged the person from the water.*
>
> *After a while, people began to dread the daily inevitable recurrence; the situation demanded a solution. To decide appropriate action, the mayor called a town meeting. Much disagreement ensued, coalescing into the formation of three factions.*
>
> - *One group wanted to continue rescuing "drowners" on an informal (catch-as-catch-can) basis.*
>
> - *The second group advocated funding a lifeguard station to monitor the river for struggling swimmers in order to rescue and resuscitate them.*
>
> - *The third group liked the idea of hiring lifeguards and providing emergency care, but felt the need to do something more. They wanted to follow the river upstream to discover the source of the problem.*

The approach used by the third group is the basis of an effective stress management program. Success in managing stress depends on discovering the source of the problem, not merely alleviating stress symptoms. Though it is useful to be alert to signs of stress, and comforting to relieve painful symptoms, unless you discover the source of your stress the problem will surely recur or escalate.

Your answers to the questions that follow will give you a snapshot of exactly where your stress is coming from *at this particular time*, and how great an effect the stress is having on your overall sense of well-being right now.

These questions are grouped in scales that are collectively known as the **Personal Stress Assessment Inventory** (PSAI) and are your diagnostic instruments. They are validated by research and have been widely used for over a decade.[1]

PSAI scales have no **right** or **wrong** answers. The best answers are the most honest—how you truly are and your actual recent behavior, not how you wish you were.

We recommend that you not discuss your stress inventory profile with family members, friends or colleagues. It is personal and private. Why dissipate energy explaining your scores?

Allow yourself a half-hour or so to relax and enjoy the process of taking your *Personal Stress Assessment Inventory.*

NOTE: The *Personal Stress Assessment Inventory* may be purchased from the Center For Management Effectiveness, P.O. Box 1202, Pacific Palisades, CA 90272, (310) 459-6052.

SCALE I: PREDISPOSITION

DIRECTIONS: If your behavior during the past 30 days was more like the **left-hand** statement, circle a number between 1 and 5, where 1 describes your most consistent behavior. If your behavior during the past 30 days was more like the **right-hand** statement, circle a number between 6 and 10, where 10 describes your most consistent behavior. Circle only one number for each pair of contrasting statements.

a. I rarely got irritated when things didn't go my way.   1 2 3 4 5 6 7 8 9 10   I often got irritated when things didn't go my way.

b. I often got annoyed when I waited in line.   1 2 3 4 5 6 7 8 9 10   I rarely got annoyed when I waited in line.

c. I rarely felt that people were selfish or insensitive.   1 2 3 4 5 6 7 8 9 10   I often felt that people were selfish or insensitive.

d. I often felt that people who got in my way were pushy or inconsiderate.   1 2 3 4 5 6 7 8 9 10   I rarely felt that people who got in my way were pushy or inconsiderate.

e. I rarely "put words into another person's mouth" to speed things up.   1 2 3 4 5 6 7 8 9 10   I often "put words into another person's mouth" to speed things up.

f. I often compared my performance to others'.   1 2 3 4 5 6 7 8 9 10   I rarely compared my performance to others'.

g. I rarely took the success of others as a challenge.   1 2 3 4 5 6 7 8 9 10   I often took the success of others as a challenge.

h. My self-esteem often depended on what I accomplished.   1 2 3 4 5 6 7 8 9 10   My self-esteem rarely depended on what I accomplished.

i. It was rarely difficult for me to leave my work at the office.   1 2 3 4 5 6 7 8 9 10   It was often difficult for me to leave my work at the office.

j. I often pushed myself when I felt tired.   1 2 3 4 5 6 7 8 9 10   I rarely pushed myself when I felt tired.

Transfer the numbers you circled above to the appropriate column below and calculate your Predisposition Score.

Column 1	Column 2	SCORING
a. _____	b. _____	55
c. _____	d. _____	+ _____ Column 1 Total
e. _____	f. _____	= _____ **Subtotal**
g. _____	h. _____	− _____ Column 2 Total
i. _____	j. _____	= _____ **Grand Total**
		Divide Grand Total by 10
Total Column 1	**Total Column 2**	☐ **Your Predisposition Score**

SCALE II: RESILIENCE

FREQUENTLY	OCCASIONALLY	RARELY	NOT IN LAST 30 DAYS	
				DIRECTIONS: Please respond to *each* of the following statements. Circle a number in the column that best describes your behavior during the past 30 days or so. Unless noted otherwise, score "frequently," as once a week or more often; "occasionally," somewhat less than once a week; and "rarely," less than occasionally. Score all items.
1	2	3	4	a. I engage in creative activities (such as art, writing, music, etc.) outside of work.
1	2	3	4	b. I meditate or focus my attention inwardly without interruption. (Frequently means daily.)
1	2	3	4	c. I participate in sustained, rhythmic "aerobic" exercise. (Frequently means at least every other day.)
1	2	3	4	d. I write about my thoughts and feelings and reflect upon them.
1	2	3	4	e. I seek places where I can find serenity.
1	2	3	4	f. I avoid the use of tobacco. (Frequently avoid is not smoking at all; Occasionally is less than one pack a week.)
1	2	3	4	g. I avoid the use of liquor. (Frequently avoid is consuming less than 6 ounces per week of liquor or equivalent amounts of wine and beer.)
1	2	3	4	h. I treat myself to meaningful rewards.
1	2	3	4	i. I find serenity in spiritual activity or contemplation.
1	2	3	4	j. I maintain my weight at a level that feels ideal to me.
1	2	3	4	k. I spend time thinking about what is important to me.
1	2	3	4	l. I eat whole-grain foods and raw fruits and fresh vegetables and avoid adding salt and sugar to foods. (Frequently is daily.)
1	2	3	4	m. I let the appropriate people know when I feel overloaded, and I say "no" when I mean it.
1	2	3	4	n. I avoid caffeine.
1	2	3	4	o. I release body tension through breathing exercises or some form of systematic stretching or yoga. (Frequently is at least every other day.)
1	2	3	4	p. I confide in friends and family to whom I also express my feelings, including love and anger.
1	2	3	4	q. I engage in noncompetitive, play-type activities. (Frequently is daily.) Examples: hobbies, kite flying, dancing, playing with pets.
1	2	3	4	r. I ask for, and receive, affection or emotional support from friends and family.
1	2	3	4	s. I am satisfied with the quality and frequency of my sexual life.
1	2	3	4	t. I use car safety devices. (Frequently is every opportunity.)
				TOTAL SCORE **SCORING** 1. Add the numbers you circled in each of the four columns, and write these subtotals in the box below each column. 2. Add the subtotals and write in your total score.

SCALE III-A: STRESS SOURCES—Periodic, Personal

EMOTIONAL IMPACT SCORE	**DIRECTIONS:** For each event that occurred at any time in the past, score your *present* emotional impact (i.e., from "1" low impact to "10" major impact). "Emotional impact" is the force that tends to disturb your emotional balance or equilibrium, or the energy you require to get back to "feeling normal." Score items that aren't applicable, or that have no present emotional impact on you as "0."
_____	a. A person close to me died.
_____	b. I or a person close to me ended or changed the nature of our relationship.
_____	c. A family member created problems for me.
_____	d. I had an injury, accident, illness or was a crime victim.
_____	e. I got married, had a reconciliation or entered a new close relationship.
_____	f. I started to experience sexual or emotional difficulties.
_____	g. A person close to me had a change of health, or started having an alcohol, drug or eating problem.
_____	h. My spouse or I, experienced problems involving pregnancy.
_____	i. A new family member was added (include adopting, a relative moving in, or birth of a grandchild).
_____	j. I was involved with litigation or credit problems.
_____	k. A son, daughter or other relative left or returned home.
_____	l. I obtained or was denied a mortgage or loan.
_____	m. I had trouble with friends or neighbors.
_____	n. A family member started or stopped working.
_____	o. I changed smoking, drinking or eating habits.
_____	p. My expenses or income greatly changed.
_____	q. I had a financial reversal, loss, theft or damage to personal property.
_____	r. I changed my residence.
_____	s. I changed my usual recreational, social, educational or religious activities.
_____	t. I made a major decision about my future.
	If not covered above, write in one or two emotionally unsettling experiences below.
_____	u. _____
_____	v. _____
	TOTAL SCORE (Please write in the column total.)

SCALE III-B: STRESS SOURCES—Periodic, Work-Related

EMOTIONAL IMPACT SCORE	**DIRECTIONS:** Please complete this page following the directions given on page 39.
_____	a. I lost my job, retired or may soon lose my job.
_____	b. I was transferred to a new location, position or assignment, or was involved in a reorganization.
_____	c. I was passed over for promotion.
_____	d. I was criticized by my boss.
_____	e. I criticized others, or argued with an employee.
_____	f. The nature of my work or activity level significantly changed.
_____	g. I received a salary adjustment different from my expectation.
_____	h. I fired, transferred or laid-off an employee.
_____	i. A valued co-worker was transferred, retired or terminated.
_____	j. I hired, or was assigned, one or more new employees.
_____	k. My job performance review was disturbing.
_____	l. Major policy or procedural changes occurred.
_____	m. I was assigned a new boss.
_____	n. Working hours or conditions changed.
_____	o. I experienced discomfort in reviewing the job performance of others.
_____	p. I gave a talk, or made a presentation to a group.
_____	q. A decision affecting me was made without consulting me or asking for my comments.
_____	r. I started or ended a difficult educational or training program.
_____	s. My request for a change in assignment was denied or delayed.
_____	t. Work interfered with my personal or social life.
	If not covered above, write in one or two emotionally unsettling experiences below.
_____	u. _____
_____	v. _____
	TOTAL SCORE (Please write in the column total.)

SCALE III-C: STRESS SOURCES—Continuing, Personal

EMOTIONAL IMPACT SCORE		DIRECTIONS: For each event that occurred during the past 30 days, indicate your emotional impact score ("1" low impact, to "10" major impact). After you have assessed the emotional impact (for example, assume you judged a "6" impact) then place the 6 in either column A or B, whichever is applicable. Alternatively, you may divide your score between columns A and B (for example, scoring "4" in column A and "2" in column B). Score items that aren't applicable, or that have no present emotional impact on you as "0."
Events Beyond My Power To Change	Events Within My Power To Change	
Column A	Column B	

Column A	Column B	
_____	_____	a. One or more dependents present continuing problems.
_____	_____	b. I lack adequate privacy.
_____	_____	c. I don't feel close to, or in touch with, parents or other family members.
_____	_____	d. Traffic congestion, commuting, or related problems are difficult.
_____	_____	e. I don't have enough friends I feel close to and can count on.
_____	_____	f. I feel my home is too noisy, messy or not as safe or comfortable as I would like.
_____	_____	g. I don't feel as healthy as I would like.
_____	_____	h. I don't have enough intimacy or satisfaction in my primary relationship.
_____	_____	i. Pollution (including smog, noise, smoke and impure water) is annoying or irritating.
_____	_____	j. Family members have chronic health or addictive problems.
_____	_____	k. Money is a continuing worry, such as rising expenses, investment concerns, my children's education, preparing for my own retirement, etc.
_____	_____	l. My lifestyle lacks excitement, or doesn't serve my deepest needs.
_____	_____	m. My life is taken up with too many responsibilities (such as paperwork, household tasks and repairs).
_____	_____	n. I feel under-appreciated at home, or elsewhere in my personal life.
_____	_____	o. The relationships, activities or work schedules of my spouse or close friends create continuing problems.
_____	_____	p. I am concerned about the general economic, political, law-enforcement, military, terrorism, or moral situation in this country and elsewhere.
_____	_____	q. I use too much energy to please others.
_____	_____	r. Expressing my feelings—such as anger, sadness and love—is difficult for me.
_____	_____	s. I don't have enough quality time with my family, or for personal leisure and enjoyment.
_____	_____	t. Recreational, social, educational or religious facilities or babysitters are inadequate or too far away, or inconveniently scheduled for me or my family.
		If not covered above, write in one or two emotionally unsettling experiences below.
_____	_____	u. _____
_____	_____	v. _____

Column A TOTAL	Column B TOTAL	
_____	_____	**TOTAL SCORE** _____ Sum of Columns A and B

SCALE III-D: STRESS SOURCES—Continuing, Work-Related

EMOTIONAL IMPACT SCORE		DIRECTIONS: Please complete this page following the directions given on page 41.
Events Beyond My Power To Change	Events Within My Power To Change	
Column A	Column B	

Column A	Column B	
_____	_____	a. Job security or my future with my employer is a continuing problem.
_____	_____	b. I'm not clear what's expected of me; or what is expected is unreasonable.
_____	_____	c. I am bored with my job.
_____	_____	d. Dealing with others (including co-workers, customers, clients, vendors) creates relationship problems (such as office politics, discrimination, rivalry, or sexual harassment).
_____	_____	e. My work is interrupted too often, or the demands of others on my time is burdensome.
_____	_____	f. I have too little authority or lack training to carry out my responsibilities effectively.
_____	_____	g. I feel my performance is not judged properly (e.g., I mostly get feedback when something goes wrong; standards aren't clear; or, there's favoritism).
_____	_____	h. I haven't enough input to, or involvement with, decisions that seriously affect me.
_____	_____	i. I'm not satisfied with my compensation or benefits.
_____	_____	j. I feel overloaded by deadline pressure or frequent crises.
_____	_____	k. I'm not advancing in my career in the direction or at the pace I would like.
_____	_____	l. I'm not satisfied with upper management's performance or support.
_____	_____	m. My employees are not as well motivated as I would like.
_____	_____	n. I attend meetings that waste my time.
_____	_____	o. I don't feel my performance is adequately recognized.
_____	_____	p. Giving negative feedback to others creates difficulties.
_____	_____	q. I have too much or not enough interaction with others, or too few friendships at work.
_____	_____	r. Work situations create moral or ethical problems.
_____	_____	s. I am involved with too much or not enough travel.
_____	_____	t. I experience too many system problems (e.g., inadequate resources, equipment, facilities or procedures).
		If not covered above, write in one or two emotionally unsettling experiences below.
_____	_____	u. _____
_____	_____	v. _____

Column A TOTAL	Column B TOTAL	
_____	_____	**TOTAL SCORE** _____ Sum of Columns A and B

SCALE IV: HEALTH SYMPTOMS

DIRECTIONS: Please respond to each of the following statements. *Circle a number* in the column that best describes your body symptoms or your feelings during the past *30 days*. Score "frequently" as once a week or more often; "occasionally" as somewhat less than once a week; and "rarely" as less than occasionally. Score all items.

FREQUENTLY	OCCASIONALLY	RARELY	NOT IN LAST 30 DAYS	PHYSICAL SYMPTOMS	FREQUENTLY	OCCASIONALLY	RARELY	NOT IN LAST 30 DAYS	PSYCHOLOGICAL SYMPTOMS
4	2	1	0	a. Headaches, mild or severe.	4	2	1	0	1. Difficulty getting to sleep or staying asleep.
4	2	1	0	b. Other aches, pains or cramps.	4	2	1	0	2. Frightening dreams.
4	2	1	0	c. Cold or flu.	4	2	1	0	3. Hard to get up mornings.
4	2	1	0	d. Allergies or hay fever.	4	2	1	0	4. Nervous habits like tapping fingers or grinding teeth.
4	2	1	0	e. Skin rash or itching.					
4	2	1	0	f. Loss of appetite.	4	2	1	0	5. Difficulty concentrating or easily distracted.
4	2	1	0	g. Upset stomach, nausea or stomach ache.	4	2	1	0	6. Emotional outbursts or blaming others.
					4	2	1	0	7. Used pain-killer, sedative or tranquilizer.
4	2	1	0	h. Excess gas or heartburn.	4	2	1	0	8. Nervous around authorities (like top executives).
4	2	1	0	i. Constipation.					
4	2	1	0	j. Diarrhea.	4	2	1	0	9. Easily startled, irritated or upset.
4	2	1	0	k. Urgent or excessive need to urinate.	4	2	1	0	10. Fearful of certain things, events, or activities.
4	2	1	0	l. Dryness of throat or mouth, or laryngitis.	4	2	1	0	11. Hurt by criticism, feeling self-critical or guilty.
					4	2	1	0	12. Easily discouraged, or nothing seems important.
4	2	1	0	m. Heart beating hard or faster than usual, or palpitations.	4	2	1	0	13. Increased eating, smoking, alcohol, coffee, drugs or gambling.
4	2	1	0	n. Trouble getting breath.					
4	2	1	0	o. Sweating or clammy even when temperature is cool.	4	2	1	0	14. Feel helpless, out of control or overwhelmed.
					4	2	1	0	15. Feel blue, under the weather, or gloomy.
4	2	1	0	p. Hot or cold spells.	4	2	1	0	16. Keyed up, jittery, or stewing about things.
4	2	1	0	q. Faintness, dizziness, twitches, tics or trembling.	4	2	1	0	17. Low energy level, withdrawing from others or diminished sexual desire.
				If not covered above, add one or two body symptoms that you attribute to stress.					*If not covered above, add one or two psychological symptoms that you attribute to stress.*
4	2	1	0	r. _____	4	2	1	0	18. _____
4	2	1	0	s. _____	4	2	1	0	19. _____
		0	=	**TOTAL PHYSICAL SYMPTOMS**			0	=	**TOTAL PSYCHOLOGICAL SYMPTOMS**

SCORING:
1. Add the circled numbers in each column, and write these subtotals below each column.
2. Write in your total physical symptoms and your total psychological symptoms. Add the two together and write your total health symptoms score here: **TOTAL HEALTH SYMPTOMS**

CHAPTER 6

UNDERSTANDING YOUR STRESS SCORES

The scores you calculated in Chapter 5 are essential to the foundation of your stress management program. To design a responsive action plan, you need to know what each scale is intended to measure and what the numbers mean. When your scores deviate from the statistical norms given in this chapter, it is a signal that you may be over- or underreacting to events in your life. Consider this as opportunity to explore further.

Scale I: Predisposition

What This Scale Is Designed to Measure

Your Predisposition score is related to the "Type A" behavior pattern characterized by three key factors: time urgency, aggressive competitiveness and hostility. Unlike hostility, rushing and competing are not inherently Type A behaviors. Only the *automatic, unconscious* drive to rush and compete are of concern.

► **Time Urgency**
  Type A's are driven by an inner push to do more-and-more in less-and-less time regardless of whether or not the situation requires haste. They have difficulty simply waiting, and define relaxing as wasting time.

► **Aggressive Competitiveness**
  Type A's fight to win and keep on winning, as though life itself were a competitive event. When teaching a four-year-old nephew how to play checkers, an adult Type A couldn't keep from trying for a big win.

► **Hostility**
  Type A's are easily irritated and excessively critical of anyone who gets in their way.

The Predisposition scale measures hostility indirectly, because most people do not allow themselves to be aware of their own hostile attitudes or behavior. Ironically, hostility is obvious to everyone except the person acting in a hostile manner.

The authors of *Treating Type A Behavior and Your Heart*, Meyer Friedman and Diane Ulmer, asked a participant in their program if his hostility had diminished during the year he had been in the program. Without a moment's hesitation, he answered:

> "I do not believe I have excess hostility; this is due in part to the fact that my intellectual, physical and cultural attributes surpass 98 percent of the bastards I have to deal with.

> "Furthermore, those dome-head, fitness-freak, goody-good types that make up the alleged 2 percent, I could beat in a second if I weren't so damn busy fighting every minute to keep that 98 percent from trying to walk over me."[1]

High Predisposition scores are indicators of a Type A pattern of hostility, because the relentless need to rush and compete sets up many opportunities to be frustrated. Individuals with high scores should consider asking close friends for feedback and practice nonjudgmental self-observation for signs of hostility patterns.

What the Numbers Mean

Predisposition scores *above 7.0,* especially when coupled with a hot temper or *short fuse*, indicate your behavior pattern may be increasing your risk of cardiovascular disease. Low scores have no adverse impact.

Refer to Chapter 7, "Overcoming Type A Predisposition" for ideas on how to reduce an excessively high score.

Scale II: Resilience

What This Scale Is Designed to Measure

Resilience is "the ability to recover from or readily adjust to misfortune or change." The Resilience scale measures your ability to recover your balance following any event that upsets you.

What the Numbers Mean

Your Resilience score indicates how well you bounce back from life's pressures and adversities. Resilience scores *higher than 50* indicate your life is currently out of balance, making you vulnerable to illness in the face of life's changing demands. You are likely to experience difficulty recovering from continuous or frequently recurring stress. Chapter 8 offers guidelines for creating greater balance.

Scale III-A & III-B: Periodic Stress Sources—Personal and Work-Related

What This Scale Is Designed to Measure

This scale measures change and the level of emotional impact intermittent changes are having on your life. Your score reflects how much adaptive energy you deplete attempting to maintain equilibrium.

What the Numbers Mean

If you scored *above 50* on either Scale III-A or III-B, you may be feeling drained or overwhelmed. Refer to Chapter 9 for ideas on how to protect yourself from illness or injury, and replenish your energy while dealing with life changes.

On the other hand, if you scored *below 10* on either scale, you may be denying the emotional impact important events are having on your life. Or, assuming your scores accurately reflect your emotional response, you may be risk-averse and missing opportunities for adventure and growth.

Research Related to Illness and Life Events

The relationship between illness and life events was developed in the 1930's by Adolph Meyer, who designed the "life chart" linking disease and life changes. Meyer's idea was expanded by Thomas Holmes and Richard Rahe, who designed the Social Readjustment Rating Scale, which assigned numerical values called Life Change Units (LCU) to life events.

Their scale had *two drawbacks*:

1. The LCUs had statistical validity for an "average" person, not a specific individual. For example, in a divorce, both people were assigned the same number even though one partner may have been more upset by the breakup.

2. The scale dealt only with one year of prior personal history. If a parent died thirteen months before the test was taken, no points were scored, even though the event might still have a profound emotional impact.

The scales you completed have *two advantages*:

1. You did not use an abstract statistical average, but rather scored how you actually felt.

2. You were not limited to any time period when scoring the Stress Sources scales. You took a current "snapshot," irrespective of when stress-evoking events occurred, giving you a current assessment that integrates all past upsets.

Scale III-C & III-D: Continuing Stress Sources— Personal and Work-Related

What This Scale Is Designed to Measure

The insidious wear-and-tear from day in, day out continuing stress makes you vulnerable to chronic, degenerative illness. This scale measures the level of emotional impact that you experience from ongoing stress triggers.

Additionally, the scores you assigned as *beyond* and *within* your power to change reflect the degree to which you see yourself empowered or a victim of circumstance. Your health is less at risk when you perceive yourself as having the power to "disarm" a stress trigger.[2]

What the Numbers Mean

If your score is *above 50* on either Scale III-C or III-D, your emotional response to present events is an *important distress signal*. The need to continually cope with your discontent saps vital energy reserves.

On the other hand, if you scored *below 10* on either scale, you may be out of touch with your feelings. Or, assuming your scores accurately reflect your emotional response, you have an opportunity to add spice and zest to your life by taking more chances, breaking out of familiar patterns and challenging yourself to reach for peak performance.

A crucial aspect of this scale is how you scored events you see as "beyond my power to change" (*external*) and "within my power to change" (*internal*). If your score is *10 points or higher* in the external column, you see yourself without adequate control over the everyday events in your life. This perception leads to burnout. Researchers Ayala Pines and Elliot Aronson identified the three key elements of burnout: feelings of helplessness, hopelessness and entrapment.[3] Some cancer patients also describe their lives, before diagnosis of their illness, as helpless and hopeless, and say they felt like victims of circumstance.[4] If your score indicates a tendency to perceive sources of stress as remaining beyond your power to change, Chapter 10 will be helpful.

Scale IV: Health Symptoms

What This Scale Is Designed to Measure

This scale indicates how often during the past month you experienced a wide variety of stress-related physical and psychological symptoms.

What the Numbers Mean

Total scores *above 40* suggest excessive stress and the need to develop an effective stress management program. (They also suggest that you would do well to have a medical checkup.) The chapters that follow will guide you in designing a program tailored to your individual needs.

If your total score is *above 40* and *physical* symptoms are *10 or more points higher* than your psychological symptoms, exercise is recommended as a component of your overall program.[5] A physical checkup is advisable before starting any program of vigorous exercise. If your total score is *above 40* and *psychological* symptoms are *10 or more points higher* than your somatic symptoms, deep relaxation is recommended. Also consider talking with a psychotherapist. Relaxation methods and physical fitness are discussed in Chapters 14 and 16.

Review

Your Personal Action Options

UNDERSTANDING YOUR STRESS SCORES

1. Review your scores.
Reflect on the behavior you exhibit and try to modify your stress reactions.

2. Modify Type A Behavior
See Chapter 7 for methods of overcoming Type A behavior.

PART THREE

MANAGING YOUR STRESS

"*If only I had known I was going to live so long I would have taken better care of myself.*"

—Anonymous

CHAPTER 7

OVERCOMING TYPE A PREDISPOSITION

The purpose of this chapter is to reduce your chances of having a heart attack or stroke. *Everyone* can benefit from this review because we live in a society that rewards Type A behavior. We are all at risk. If you scored *above 7.0* on the Predisposition scale, your vulnerability is greater than average.

Recall from Chapter 6 that Type A behavior has three components: **time urgency, aggressive competitiveness,** and **hostility.** There are times when the conscious choice to rush and compete are appropriate, but it is the *compulsivity* of Type A behavior, and the *hostility* component evoked by mindless rushing and pushing, that puts your health at risk.[1]

> *An important point about language: People are not Type A's. Type A behavior is just that—behavior, and it can be changed. Because the authors refer so often to the Type A behavior pattern, for shorthand we refer to people who currently act that way as "Type A's" or simply "A's."*

A's Underlying Belief System

Common to people who exhibit Type A behavior is a fundamental belief that self-worth is not a given and must be continually re-earned. Their personal worth is always at stake, forcing them to keep striving to achieve. A's drive themselves relentlessly. Enough is never enough.

In contrast, "Type B's" do not question their self-worth. They don't put energy into proving their value, since they take for granted that they are worthy. Type B's tell us: "It never occurs to me that my self-worth is at stake."

The key to changing Type A behavior and, paradoxically, having more energy to be effective in what you do, is to appreciate that you already *are* a worthy person. Self-worth does not depend on *doing*; it is a quality of *being*.

We make an important distinction between self-esteem, which is based on behavior, and self-worth, the intrinsic value of a human being, which we believe is everyone's birthright.

The Link between Type A Behavior and Coronary Heart Disease

The greater your compulsive need to rush or win, the more often you will trigger the fight-or-flight response. Continually tripping your stress alarm burdens the heart. A's increase the likelihood of triggering the fight-or-flight response with each of their three characteristic behavior patterns.

Time Urgency

If you feel you can "never catch up," the compulsion to rush will be strong. Type A's have an insatiable need to save time. They attempt several activities such as talking on the phone, reading their mail and watching television, all at the same time. You can spot a Type A darting in and out of traffic to save three car lengths.

> *A woman told the story about a six-day honeymoon in Venice with her Type A husband, a high-powered Beverly Hills attorney. He phoned his secretary twice a day for messages and handled urgent business from the bridal suite. On their last evening in Venice, as they were returning from a day of sight-seeing, his wife suggested stopping for a cappuccino to enjoy a romantic moment at sunset. Her husband exploded, "I can't afford to waste the time; don't you realize what time zone we're in? I'll barely be able to get back to the hotel to phone an important client!"*

The attorney saw nothing odd about his behavior. In fact, he felt he was doing his wife a favor working the honeymoon into his busy schedule—it was his first week off in ten years.

Unfortunately, short of leaving the marriage, there is little this woman can do until the need to change becomes important enough to her husband for him to want to overcome his automatic pattern.

Aggressive Competitiveness

Type A's must win. Driving themselves relentlessly, they prepare to compete as though mobilizing for trench warfare. Terms such as "do or die" and "publish or perish" are taken literally.

Former Redskins's football coach, Vince Lombardi, became their champion when he proclaimed: "Winning isn't everything, but losing is nothing."

To keep check on how well they are doing, A's quantify whenever possible; they want to see *the numbers*. Returning from a vacation trip, A's may recount to their co-workers, "Our first full day on the road, I drove 343 miles, 375 on the second, and I got over 400 miles twice." A's also hate to stop while driving long distances; all those drivers they passed may regain the lead.

After learning about the driving habits of Type A's, a woman told this story about her father:

> *"I finally understood Dad. When I was five years old, my mother insisted we drive out West for a family vacation. After four days we reached the Grand Canyon. Dad leaped out of the automobile, ran to the Canyon's rim, and shot a roll of film. He jumped back in the car, gunned the engine, ready to leave. I pleaded, 'Daddy, I want to see the Grand Canyon.' 'Get back in the car,' he barked over his shoulder, 'I'll show you the photos when we get home!' "*

Hostility

People who are mistrustful and cynical about the motives of others often elicit hostile behavior in return—which confirms their suspicions. This makes them ever more hypervigilant, and the downward spiral becomes a self-fulfilling prophesy.

A's are certain the person ahead of them at the express check-out line exceeded the ten-item limit. Fuming behind people who cash checks and redeem coupons, Type A's are vulnerable to having a stress attack on the spot.

Constant frustration and anger overwork the heart muscle. Blood vessels constrict in peripheral body areas while the heart pumps harder. This opposing action is something like stepping simultaneously on your car's brakes and accelerator. In addition, the wear and tear on the heart muscles causes blood platelets and fatty acids to collect and build along arterial walls, causing atherosclerosis, a condition that narrows and hardens the arteries. In time, a blood clot can lodge in the narrowed artery, stopping blood flow and causing a heart attack.

Changing Type A Behavior

Don't kid yourself. A lifetime of entrenched behavior is enormously difficult to change. Societal pressure starting in kindergarten rewards superachievers.

For example, Merrill Lynch, Ernst & Young, and *Inc.* magazine, announced in full-page ads a competitive award they described as "the most prestigious recognition event for entrepreneurs." Criteria for winning are:

- Be first to arrive at work, and last to leave.

- Routinely wake up in the middle of the night to jot down ideas.

- Have an extended family called "my staff."

- Hardly remember what the sun feels like.

This event could have been called "a competition to see who can survive this invitation to a heart attack."

The MAP Strategy

To guide you in changing Type A behavior, the authors have identified a *three-step strategy*. The acronym **MAP,** which stands for **M**otivation, **A**wareness and **P**ractice, can help you to remember this strategy.

Step 1: Motivation

Do you believe any of your Type A behaviors increase your risk of heart attack? If your answer is "no," you have lots of company. Most Type A's think, "It will never happen to me," and are willing to change their habitual lifestyle only *after* a crisis. The President of the American Psychological Association, Logan Wright, reports:

> "Prior to the occurrence of a heart attack or bypass surgery, A's are notorious for denying their tendencies and for refusing to alter their lifestyles."[2]

Wright's experience is widely shared. A shock or trauma is often required to get A's motivated to change their behavior. One of our workshop participants reported rushing to get ready for an early morning airline flight. He dashed to his Porsche, threw it in reverse, and sped backward out of his driveway. Hearing his wife's piercing scream, he slammed on his brakes, missing his three-year-old child by inches. Trembling, in a cold sweat, he cautiously emerged from his automobile vowing to change his behavior from that moment on.

Spare yourself the jolt of an unnecessary life crisis. Appreciate how serious a heart attack or accident would be to yourself and others who love you. As you are rushing, occasionally raise the question to yourself, calmly,

- Is it worth the price?
- Is this situation worth making myself sick or risking death?

Step 2: Awareness

The key to cardiovascular health is conscious awareness: the ability to choose when it is appropriate to rush, and when to rest; when to be assertive, and when to back off. Compulsive unconscious Type A behaviors endanger health. Unless A's gain an *awareness of their reflexive reactions*, they remain prisoners of their behavior pattern. Fortunately, change can occur through **conscious perception, assessment** and **choice.**

The father who yelled at his daughter for delaying him at the Grand Canyon, if asked, would insist he had not intentionally expressed hostility toward his five-year-old. He might even say: "On the contrary, I make it a point to take my family on interesting vacation trips."

When Friedman and Rosenman pioneered their research, they found that nonverbal cues were essential for identifying Type A behavior.[3] Participants in these studies were asked if they were prone to anger. Those who reacted by storming, "Hell, no!" were moved up a notch on the Type A scale.

For people strongly motivated to change, awareness of their unconscious compulsion is well-served through self-observation, soliciting frank feedback from others and remaining receptive even when feedback conflicts with self-image.

Step 3: Practice

To change Type A behavior, you need to develop new patterns of thinking. With practice, you will gain confidence in using alternative behaviors. Try the following exercise to open yourself to a wider behavioral repertoire.

Exercise 7

Place a check mark next to the following statements that you could accept. These beliefs are characteristic of people with Type B behavior.

❏ I feel better and increase chances of success when I am calm and centered.

❏ I experience my power through gentleness as well as dominance, as appropriate to each situation.

❏ My life is my unfinished masterpiece; my career is just one part of my life purpose.

❏ I let myself experience feelings of vulnerability, rather than escape into activity.

❏ I don't take myself too seriously. I enjoy a good laugh at myself.

❏ I am a worthy person, deserving of love and respect. I don't have to prove my self-worth.

On index cards, write the Type B beliefs you checked; one statement to a card. In time you may be willing to add others.

Begin by selecting one card each day as your reminder. Read it upon awakening and before going to bed each night. During the days, **allow the statement to be expressed through your behavior**.

Changing deeply rooted behavior requires practice. Start small. Here are some new behaviors to consider.

- At least once each week, listen to music or read a book unrelated to your career.

- During your workday take hourly stretch breaks. Raise your arms above your head. Stretch to the right and hold for a count of five, then to the left. Repeat several times, breathing deeply.

- While eating, sit down and chew your food deliberately, tasting and enjoying each bite.

- Create friendships from which you have nothing material to gain.

- If you have young children, take some time each day to listen, giving each child your undivided rapt attention.

- Play a game for sheer enjoyment, without keeping score.

- Slow down and breathe consciously.

One of our workshop attendees recently reported how he shifted his Type A behavior commuting to work. Previously, he saw other drivers as the enemy competing to be the lead car. He now graciously invites eager drivers to cut in ahead of him. His rewards outweigh the few minutes he loses in traffic. He arrives at his destination feeling relaxed rather than frazzled, and enjoys the surprised and pleased responses from his fellow drivers.

Discussing your new experiences with others in mutual support groups can be extremely helpful. Courage and perseverance are needed to confront deeply rooted beliefs and attitudes. Use the structure of the **MAP** strategy to guide you in overcoming automatic Type A behaviors.

When you notice yourself feeling unnecessarily tense or rushed, take a few slow, deep breaths. Let all the tension flow out of your arms and legs. Softly say to yourself "RELAX." You will live long enough to see the quality of your life improve.

Review

> *Your Personal Action Options*
>
> ## OVERCOMING TYPE A PREDISPOSITION
>
> 1. **Change beliefs about self-worth.**
>   Experiment with the statement: "I am a worthy person; I do not need to prove my self-worth."
>
> 2. **Let go of having to win.**
>   See Chapter 13 for ideas about "letting go."

CHAPTER 8

BUILDING RESILIENCE

Resilience is the ability to spring back from whatever pitfalls life has to offer. It allows you to deal with impossible schedules, unfair rules and difficult people, without losing yourself or impairing your health.

We are born with natural resilience. Toddlers fall when learning to walk. Within a few minutes, the tragedy is over and the child is ready to try again. What happens to this precious ability? As years go by, resilience decreases through unbalanced living and the inevitable process of aging.

The essence of resilience is dynamic balance.

Before proceeding with this chapter, it may be helpful to review the Resilience scale in Chapter 5.

The Reaching-Centering Principle

Life has an ebb and flow that needs to be recognized and honored. It is a rhythm of reaching out into the world and bringing the external experience back to your inner center to be assimilated. Whenever this natural process is interrupted, or we remain too long in either the *reaching* or *centering* phase, we feel stuck and stressed.

▶ **Reaching**
In daily life, reaching translates to initiating, asserting, experimenting, exploring and stretching. It is that part of the creative cycle where you stick your neck out and innovate. Reaching requires risking the security of your present position to keep moving into new terrain. It is outer-world oriented.

Child psychologist Jean Piaget captured the spirit of reaching: "Development involves the active process of the organism *ever* reaching out to incorporate new experience within the limits permitted by its capacities."[1]

► **Centering**

Centering occurs in "a place in which activities concentrate and from which something new originates." It is the digesting of outer experience that enables us to move to the next level of development or discovery. Each new experience has a tentative quality, like a photographic print in its developing solution. While soaking, the full picture emerges. Centering is the process by which you come to know your essential self—your center of being.

From the experience of centering, you create an inner stability that naturally prepares you to reach out for new stimulation. Ira Progoff notes:

> "Whenever a phase of our life completes itself, and we reach a particular level of achievement and awareness, that, in turn becomes our new starting point. All those life difficulties that we might otherwise think of as problems become the raw material of our new development."[2]

Understanding the flow between reaching and centering can help you maintain harmony between your outer and inner worlds, between seeking company and solitude, between striving and simply being.

Balancing Four Basic Human Dimensions

As we move through life, most of us develop a preference for one or two of the four basic human dimensions (mental, emotional, physical and spiritual) at the expense of the other dimensions.

- Mental people often neglect their bodies.

- Emotional people tend to ignore logic and rationality.

- Physical people can be insensitive to feelings.

- Spiritual people may avoid interpersonal difficulties or sensuality.

To be resilient, we need to be responsive in all four areas.

Of the 20 items on the Chapter 5 Resilience scale, which do you imagine are the activities least frequently engaged in by respondents, regardless of age or sex? If you guessed "pursuing spiritual interests" and "showing affection," you are correct. Our society is more goal oriented and materialistic than spiritual. We are taught to value rationality and logic above emotional truths that reflect vulnerability. Ironically, sharing feelings of vulnerability with friends and trusted colleagues increases resilience over the more brittle *stiff-upper-lip* stance.

Review the Resilience scale you completed in Chapter 5, which incorporates the four basic dimensions, as illustrated by the following statements:

Physical: "I engage in sustained, rhythmic exercise."

Mental: "I spend time thinking about what is important to me."

Emotional: "I ask for and receive affection or emotional support from friends and family."

Spiritual: "I seek places where I can find serenity."

Where you scored "rarely" or "not in the last 30 days," ask yourself how your life would be better balanced if you paid more attention to these neglected activities. They are your cutting edge for future growth.

Using Affirmations

Affirmations can help you realize and reinforce desired changes. An affirmation is a positive thought stated with clarity and conviction to evoke a desired result. To affirm is to "make firm" what is in your mind as a concept or image. Affirmations are a tool for changing deeply rooted attitudes and mind sets.

Personal affirmations are most effective when you

► **Affirm in the present tense.**
"I am in excellent health" is more affirming than "My health will improve."

► **Affirm the positive.**
"I am on time for appointments" is preferable to "I am going to stop being late."

► **Affirm only for yourself.**
   Even if we knew what would be best for another person, we couldn't change their behavior. It's difficult enough to change our own. However, as you change, you may find others relating to you differently.

► **Affirm only what you truly believe is possible.**

► **Keep your affirmations specific and to the point.**

To design affirmations that will help you move in a desired direction, consider the following ten possibilities adapted from the Resilience scale of the Personal Stress Assessment Inventory.

   1. I am creative.

   2. I enjoy physical exercise.

   3. I am playful and fun to be with.

   4. I appreciate leisure time in nature.

   5. I treat myself with kindness.

   6. I find serenity in spiritual activity or contemplation.

   7. I maintain the weight that is best for me.

   8. I have all the time I need for thinking about what is important to me.

   9. I respect my own and others' boundaries.

   10. I give and receive emotional support.

Affirmations may sometimes evoke an uncomfortable body sensation or emotional reaction. This response signals that some early programming does not align with your current adult thinking and may need updating. Consider an outside perspective, perhaps with a therapist, to ferret out early programming that now works against your current intentions.

Review

> ### *Your Personal Action Options*
> ### BUILDING RESILIENCE
>
> 1. **Spend more time in activities that uplift your spirit.**
>
> 2. **Give and receive more affection.**
>   Begin with one hug a day. Hug etiquette requires asking first. "May I have a hug?" or "Would you like a hug?"
>
> 3. **Play.**
>   Try noncompetitive activities such as juggling, dancing or kite flying.
>
> 4. **Laugh.**
>   Laughing melts stress; even smiling improves digestion. Consider posting this bathroom mirror sign: "Don't take this person too seriously."
>
> 5. **Use affirmations.**
>   Reread your affirmations regularly.

CHAPTER 9

DEALING WITH LIFE CHANGES

Can you think of any emotional pain in your life that was not caused by change? The most difficult changes are those that arrive unannounced or cluster in rapid-fire succession. Where life changes include major losses, they often evoke feelings of anger, guilt and loneliness, after the initial shock.

Once disbelief and denial subside, you may be flooded with emotions. Only after a necessary grieving and healing period will you be able to let go of the loss over time, and eventually adjust to your new reality. Whether in response to major losses or multiple changes, adjustment and adaptation drains energy—energy that is not available to assist in the body's normal self-protective functions.

If you scored more than 50 on either of the Periodic Stress scales, you are most likely feeling bombarded. Although you cannot undo events that have already occurred, you need to recognize how vulnerable you are at this critical time and protect yourself against future illness and accidents.

Four Life-Change Strategies

► **Be gentle with yourself.**
   When changes pile up, we often feel fragile. Adjusting to new conditions requires a more gentle pace. Take all the time you need to absorb the shocks and replenish your energy.

► Allow adequate time between new commitments.

If you have been thinking of starting a demanding graduate program, for example, and you are aware of life-change overload, consider deferring enrollment. On the other hand, if you have an opportunity to participate in a joyful experience, go for it. Keeping your life in balance is the key to getting through rough spots with resilience.

► Anticipate life changes.

Warning signals, sometimes blatant and other times subtle, often precede change. Looking back, can you think of any hints or clues that foreshadowed unexpected changes in your life?

Adversity can better be taken in stride when the affected person is warned of a likely setback. Social psychologists call this preparatory information *emotional inoculation*. It helps the person cope with the stress-evoking event when it does occur, by mitigating shock and providing time to make adjustments or contingency plans.

Emotional inoculation is a reciprocal strategy. Alert yourself to warning signs and, when feasible, give others advance notice. A management axiom is: "Don't surprise your boss, especially with bad news."

Yale University's Irving Janis found that executives experience less pain when a decision backfires if they were well-informed of the risks in advance.[1]

► Go with the flow.

Life is not predictable, and the most disruptive changes come unannounced, often as a shock or keen disappointment. The story on the facing page, of a married couple on an unusual trip illustrates the value of simply "going with the flow."

Arthur and Janet, professors of management, had been planning a trip to India for three years. The husband-and-wife team departed, itinerary in hand, for a five-city tour during the Christmas semester break. At a stopover in Frankfurt, they were unexpectedly told that their visas were not in order. At first, they thought the German penchant for precise paperwork was the issue, which would be easily overcome with a phone call to Bombay. After numerous calls to both U.S. and Indian embassies, the weary couple conceded they were going to be stranded in the Frankfurt airport on Christmas Eve.

Still in shock, with two nonrefundable round-trip tickets to Los Angeles and nowhere to go but back home, Janet and Arthur were filled with embarrassment and self-doubt. They realized they had to turn their situation around, or it would quickly deteriorate into blaming themselves and each other for some gross stupidity, large financial loss and missed adventure. Determined not to see their situation as a desperate calamity, they consciously decided to view their calamity as a divine gift. They worked with the affirmative idea: "Something better must be in store for us." Their gloom lifted. With fresh energy, they created a new set of options.

They succeeded in enlisting sympathetic cooperation from a kindly Lufthansa employee. After a delightful visit to Heidelberg, they embarked on a carefree, memorable adventure in Israel.

This true story has a fascinating postscript. Weeks later, Arthur and Janet learned the hotel they had booked in New Delhi burned to the ground, killing several guests.

Review

> *Your Personal Action Options*
> ## DEALING WITH LIFE CHANGES
>
> **1. Be gentle and pace yourself.**
>   If several life changes have recently occurred, defer projects where feasible. Ease the pace of daily activity. Pamper yourself with a luxurious massage, jacuzzi or sauna. Invite friends to "be there" for you. Consider visiting a special vacation hideaway.
>
> **2. Give yourself time to release personal loss.**
>   Time is a great healer. Even if your loss is not a death, give yourself time to grieve and let go.
>
> **3. Turn the source of stress around.**
>   Look for the blessing in each source of stress. Is there a way you might turn it to your advantage?

CHAPTER 10

HANDLING THE DAILY GRIND

When it is tough getting out of bed in the morning and you dread facing the day *again*, your reserve energy is being severely depleted. It's time to make some basic changes.

Guard against the temptation to minimize the seriousness of high scores for the Continuing Stress Sources scales. If you saw many events as *beyond* your power to change, and if you have been feeling this way for some time, watch out. You are a candidate for burnout or chronic illness.

Unfortunately, ongoing stress feeds on itself. It induces a feeling of helplessness that in turn lowers self-esteem, creating more stress. People with serious illnesses frequently report that before they got sick, they felt like helpless victims of external circumstance, or pawns in a life drama beyond their ability to influence.

You need not succumb to this downward spiral. You can take control. The way up and out is to acknowledge your role in creating your life as it is. Without blaming yourself, acknowledge the fact that you made choices that led to your present circumstances.

Perhaps choices you made in the past no longer serve you; new information has presented itself, unforeseen changes have taken place. This is the perfect time—the open moment—to look at what needs to be done *now* and see the events that are *within* your power to change or accept.

Exercise 8

Select a quiet time and place, take three deep breaths and settle back in your chair. Recall your personal vision (from Chapter 3) or allow a new one to emerge. Take whichever vision you find more attractive at this moment; hold it in sharp focus for about two minutes. Recall the ongoing stress that you find burdensome. See if you can contain both images—your vision and the stress-eliciting situation—simultaneously. Write any feelings, thoughts, new ideas; jot or sketch any visual images that may come to you.

To help bring stressful life situations into alignment with your vision, consider the three strategies discussed below. These strategies may be used independently, sequentially or in combination.

1. Change Your Perception

Changing your perception is a good strategy when you don't have much control or influence.

Think of how people have vastly different experiences of identical situations. S. I. Hayakawa offers this vignette:

> "Years ago, I used to notice the differences among motormen on the Indiana Avenue streetcar line in Chicago—a street often blocked by badly parked cars and huge trailer trucks backing into warehouses and maneuvering in everybody's way. Some motormen seemed to expect to be able to drive down Indiana Avenue without interruption. Every time they got blocked, they would steam up with rage, clang their bells and lean out of their cars to shout at the truck drivers. At the end of a day, these motormen must have been nervous

> *wrecks; I can imagine them coming home at the end of a day, jittery and hypertensive, a menace to their wives and children.*
>
> *Other motormen, however, seemed to expect Indiana Avenue to be heavily blocked—a realistic expectation, because it usually was. They could sit and wait without impatience, calmly whistling or writing their reports."*[1]

Reframing puts an old situation in a new light. In the last chapter, the two management professors on their way to India deliberately chose to perceive their disastrous mishap as a *divine gift*. In so doing, they completely transformed their experience from a dismal failure to a successful vacation adventure.

Whenever you change your perception of an event, you also change your stress response. You can reduce excessive stress by looking at a situation through a different filter—a different belief system or expectation. The real challenge is to be flexible enough to *alter your perception* when a situation is not working for you.

2. Address the Problem Directly

To *address* means to deal *head on* with a situation; and it need not be an adversarial bout. Often, you can turn your stress around using a collaborative, problem-solving approach. When people with a common problem confer candidly without blaming, the best outcomes often occur.

Here's an illustration of how this strategy can work:

> *Hermione, a computer programmer just out of school, recently started a new job. She loved her work except for one problem. Every time Hermione talked with her boss, she left feeling frustrated. He kept cutting her off, breaking in to finish her sentences. His behavior had gotten so annoying that she spoke with him only when absolutely necessary. Hermione realized that she would hurt her career if she continued to avoid her boss. She couldn't see how to change her perception of the situation, and enjoyed her job too much to quit.*

She looked at what might be the worst consequence of directly confronting her boss. She might get fired. Then, she asked herself what might be the best outcome. Her boss would change his behavior.

Estimating that something between these extremes would be the probable outcome, Hermione decided to confront her boss. When they were in a private area, she asked, "Is this a good time to bring a problem to your attention? I feel my productivity is slipping because I get frustrated when we talk, so I avoid meeting with you. When we do talk, you almost always interrupt." Her boss replied, "Hermione, you are the only person I interrupt, and I wanted to find a way to talk with you about it without hurting your feelings. The fact is you speak so slowly, I get frustrated listening and can't keep myself from cutting in."

Hermione's risk paid off. She learned something about herself that she could correct. Hermione realized that although she had overcome a speech problem as a child, she continued to speak very slowly. With **motivation, awareness** and **practice,** Hermione learned to speak faster.

In deciding when to choose the "head on" strategy, ask yourself three questions:

- What is the *worst outcome* I can imagine?
- What is the *best possible outcome?*
- *How likely* are these consequences?

In general, this direct approach is appropriate when the person whose behavior creates problems for you is open-minded, trustworthy and not likely to act defensively. Choose a private place and allow adequate time for discussion. Under these circumstances, the approach is likely to relieve stress, and may enhance the relationship.

Role playing is a good way to prepare for addressing a stressful problem. Ask a friend to act the part of the other person involved and then reverse roles. Or, write a sample script using your imagination to capture the other person's point of view.

3. Exit

We saved this strategy for last because it is a strategy of last resort.

If you are considering the exit option, think about these important concerns:

- When you leave a long-standing tense situation, *your stress will go even higher,* at least in the short term.

- Do not exit until you learn as much as you can about the causes contributing to your stress.

- If you leave before you understand why you are stressed, you are likely to replicate the same stress elsewhere.

When you leave a situation that is a source of continuing pain, you create a chain of new challenges. When changing jobs, you will also need to adjust to losses, including special relationships at work and activities you enjoyed. If your new job requires relocating, your needs may conflict with those of other family members. You will have to find a new home, get reoriented, locate support resources such as doctors and dentists and make new friends.

Prepare for withdrawal symptoms after you end a meaningful relationship, even if you are the one initiating the termination.

Before you decide to leave a long-term, stress-evoking situation, try this exercise.

Exercise 9

Are you ready to use an exit strategy?
When you write "yes" to all four of the following questions, consider moving on.

_____ Are the long-term benefits you hope to gain by changing your current circumstances a worthwhile trade-off against the short-term stress you are likely to encounter?

_____ Have you taken advance measures to buffer the adverse consequences of leaving?

_____ Have you learned the lessons this situation had to teach?

_____ Do you feel resilient enough to handle the additional stress of change at this time?

To help you decide on a strategy for dealing with ongoing stress, we'd like to clarify two distinct, fundamentally different types of change:[2]

► **Incremental Change**
A step-by-step movement along an established path. Its intent is to follow precedent, doing more of the same, but better. Incremental change assumes the current system is acceptable, needing only refinements or a tune-up. It solves the problems of moving through a maze; it doesn't reconstruct maze walls.

► **Transformational Change**
A radical or root change, opening a new path. It requires changing basic beliefs and assumptions. It results in a discontinuity from the current system or paradigm, demanding a creative leap of faith.

Incremental change is a variation in *degree;* transformational change is a variation in *kind.* The risk of transformational change—moving from the known to the unknown—adds stress. Before taking this usually irreversible leap, we suggest continuing along a familiar path, taking small steps and first attempting incremental improvements. If you are clear that the system can't work or the assumptions on which it rests are no longer valid, then recruit whatever support and resources you need to move ahead with transformational change.

One final suggestion. All three strategies for dealing with continuing stress are easier to implement if you enlist the emotional support of people who care for you.

Review

Your Personal Action Options

HANDLING THE DAILY GRIND

1. **Empower yourself.**
   Ask yourself: *Is this within my power to change?* If you feel victimized by your job, boss, primary relationship, family or environment, consider these three empowering strategies:

   a. *Change your perception.* Turn your problem situation upside down. See the difficulty as an opportunity leading toward something better. Can you drop your expectations and comparisons?

   b. *Address the problem.* What are the best and worst outcomes of discussing your situation with people who can effect change? Collaboratively problem-solve, keeping the focus on mutual interests and concerns.

   c. *Exit.* If you were to leave a stress-evoking situation, what would be the costs and benefits? Set a time limit for leaving if the situation does not improve.

2. **Celebrate!**
   To keep the daily grind from wearing you down, create opportunities to transform the commonplace, give value to what is taken for granted, and change the ordinary into something special.

PART FOUR

EXTENDING AND IMPROVING YOUR LIFE

"What lies behind us and

What lies before us

are tiny matters compared to

What lies within us."

—Ralph Waldo Emerson

CHAPTER 11

MANAGING DISAGREEMENT CONSTRUCTIVELY

WIFE: I work as hard as he does and earn just as much money. He takes the garbage out and he thinks he's doing me a big personal favor.

HUSBAND: She's always tired, doesn't want to make love or dinner. The house is a mess. I'm turning into a maid. What did I get married for?

Take a seat in the front row, folks. The *fun* is about to begin. What may start innocently as "Honey, what's for dinner?" can become a free-for-all within minutes. Watch two mature adults turn into raving lunatics. How can this happen?

Every encounter with someone whose views differ from our own offers the potential for friction, bruised feelings, wasted time and foolish behavior. Is it any wonder so many people leave a disagreement suffering symptoms of stress?

Learning to handle disagreement constructively is a vital skill for stress management. Let's start with guiding principles.

Maintain Mutual Respect

As a disagreement heats up, words tend to boil over. Resist every temptation to put the other person down. It won't get you closer to a sound resolution or a satisfying relationship.

Search for Common Ground

All relationships rest on shared needs, values and goals. Find them. This common ground is the glue that will hold your relationship together while you explore the implications of your disagreement.

Listen Empathically

Listen as though you have no need to respond. To listen with empathy is to be *fully present* to the speaker's views. Resist preparing your answer; avoid making a judgment; defer even reacting. Don't discount what you hear when it conflicts with what you believe. Empathic listening conveys the message: "Your thoughts and feelings are important to me whether or not I agree with them."

Let Go of Having to Be Right

Don't waste your energy on the right-wrong game. Seek win-win solutions.

When disagreement is managed constructively, we have the opportunity to reduce excessive stress by:

- Clearing up misunderstandings
- Solving problems creatively
- Building cooperation and teamwork
- Developing authentic relationships

Managing disagreement constructively uses a systematic process of diagnosis, planning, implementation and follow-up. The following exercise enables you to experience this approach.

Exercise 10

Describe a disagreement, dispute or conflict that is or may become a source of stress for you.

_____

_____

_____

_____

_____

_____

_____

_____

_____

_____

_____

_____

_____

_____

_____

_____

_____

As each phase of the managing-disagreement process is described, you will have the opportunity to relate it to the source, or potential source, of stress in Exercise 10.

Three Phases of Resolution

Phase 1: Diagnosis

In this crucial phase, you identify key issues, listen to others, gather information, develop your initial views, decide priorities and learn who else has a stake in the outcome. Your diagnosis should examine sources of conflict.

Common Sources of Conflict

► **The same information is interpreted differently.**
Perhaps you see the new job you created for one of your employees as a golden career opportunity, while she experiences it as a threat.

► **Goals appear incompatible.**
You are buying a short-term win; your partner is investing in the future.

► **"Personal space" boundaries are violated.**
Are unscheduled visits by executives (called "management by walking around") seen as hovering or intrusive? Is physical friendliness experienced as sexual harassment?

► **Role boundaries are unclear.**
Do company socials foster team spirit, or put unfair pressure on employees to use their personal time to attend?

► **Old wounds still rankle.**
Hard feelings rooted in previously mismanaged conflict are still chafing and affect current interaction. Do people who felt demeaned or betrayed in an earlier encounter want to *even the score?*

► **The problem is not the problem.**
The "presenting" problem is only a symptom of the real underlying concern. Are you arguing over how to rearrange the deck chairs on the Titanic when the ship is sinking? Is the bickering over who takes out the garbage really about wanting more appreciation and intimacy?

Continue to explore the disagreement you outlined in Exercise 10. List the underlying sources of conflict.

_____

_____

_____

_____

_____

_____

Phase 2: Strategic Planning—Firm or Flexible; Personal or Impersonal

Individuals identified as skillful conflict managers were asked by researchers: "When your views differ from the views of others on issues of mutual concern, how do you prepare to handle such situations?"[1] Two themes emerged from their responses:

- First, they considered how *firmly* or *flexibly* they wanted to hold on to their initial point of view.

- Second, they decided how *intensely* or *impersonally* they wanted to interact with those who held divergent views.

Referring back to your disagreement, make the following two judgments as the starting point for developing your strategic plan.

1. How Firm or Flexible?

To make this judgment, consider:

- What might I gain or lose by remaining open to other perspectives?

- Would I benefit from learning other points of view?

- Have I the time to review other ideas?

With respect to this disagreement, I prefer to be:

_____ Firm _____ Moderately flexible _____ Flexible

2. How Personal or Impersonal?

Before deciding how intensely you want to be involved in this disagreement, consider:

- Is this relationship casual and transient, or do I want to sustain and develop it?

- Do I prefer to create more closeness or more social distance?

- Are boundaries clear?

With respect to this disagreement, I prefer to be

_____ Impersonal _____ Moderately personal _____ Personal

3. Which Strategy Is Appropriate?

The nine strategies shown on the following page provide you with a full repertoire, like a golfer's full bag of clubs, for handling disagreement.

Use the diagram to help you decide which strategy or blend of strategies best matches your situation. For example, if you decide that your situation calls for a firm, highly personal approach, the grid indicates that you consider a domination strategy.

Strategy Grid for Managing Differences

	INTENSITY OF INTERACTION			
highly involved		**DOMINATION** You direct, force compliance or resist.	**BARGAINING** You jointly seek means to split differences, trade off or take turns.	**COLLABORATION** You jointly problem-solve to integrate and satisfy all underlying concerns.
moderately involved		**SMOOTHING** You sell your views by accentuating similarities and downplaying differences.	**COEXISTENCE** You jointly establish a basis for both parties to pursue their differences independently.	**SUPPORTIVE RELEASE** You release the issue, stipulate any limits and provide needed support.
uninvolved		**MAINTENANCE** You postpone confronting differences or delay making changes.	**DECISION RULE** You jointly set objective rules that determine how differences will be handled.	**NONRESISTANCE** You offer no resistance to the other party's views, blending your efforts with theirs.

FLEXIBILITY OF VIEWPOINT

firm	moderately flexible	highly flexible

Choosing a strategy cannot be done by formula. Rather, the Strategy Grid and following elaboration are intended to suggest possibilities for your consideration.

► *Maintenance*

Definition: Despite disagreement, you maintain the status quo, at least for a while.

Common Saying: "Don't rock the boat."

Application: An irate customer phones and threatens to sue your company. You defer acting on the complaint, saying you will look into the matter. This gives you time to investigate and get legal counsel.

► *Smoothing*

Definition: You accentuate the positive aspects of your position, and downplay negative arguments.

Common Saying: "You get more with honey than with vinegar."

Application: Just prior to surgery, as your patient is lying on the operating table, you don't enumerate everything that could go wrong. Rather, you try to be reassuring, emphasizing the positive.

► *Domination*

Definition: Using power and influence to gain compliance with your views.

Common Saying: "Father knows best."

Application: When speed or confidentiality are critical, or the issue is too trivial to waste time discussing.

► *Decision Rule*

Definition: The joint agreement to use an objective rule or criterion (such as a lottery, seniority system, arbitration, or vote) for deciding among conflicting alternatives.

Common Saying: "Majority rules."

Application: "Let's design a system so that when overtime needs to be assigned, it can be handled quickly and will be seen as fair." A decision rule can also be used to break a bargaining stalemate.

► *Coexistence*

Definition: The joint decision to follow separate paths on a trial basis.

Common Saying: "Let's agree to disagree."

Application: When more evidence is needed, and a wrong decision could be costly. This is an interim strategy often used on a pilot or experimental basis. "Let's use both the manual and automated methods for two months to see which is better."

► *Bargaining*

Definition: Exchanging something that benefits both parties through offers and counter-offers.

Common Saying: "Half a loaf is better than none."

Application: "I'll loan you two technicians on Tuesday if we can use your computers during our peak load."

► *Non-Resistance*

Definition: Even though you disagree, you offer no resistance and help implement required action.

Common Saying: "Discretion is the better part of valor."

Application: You disagreed with your boss's last two ideas, and she went along with you. You disagree with her latest plan, but this time the issue is minor. You decide to go along to be seen as a team player.

► *Supportive Release*

Definition: Where you are in the position of greater power (e.g., boss, parent), you express your concerns, but encourage the other person to develop their initiative and learn from their own experience.

Common Saying: "Try out your wings."

Application: "Although that wouldn't be my first choice, you've been closer to the action. As long as you stay within the budget, I'll support your judgment. Let's talk about your progress in two weeks."

► *Collaboration*

Definition: An integration of views developed by candid discussion and empathic listening.

Common Saying: "Two heads are better than one."

Application: When issues are too important to be compromised, and when commitment is crucial.

With respect to your own disagreement situation in Exercise 10, choose one of the nine strategies as your first approach. Select a backup strategy as a contingency plan.

Initial Strategy _____

Backup Strategy _____

Phase 3: Implementation and Follow-up

Practice

Before you move ahead with your strategy, practice may be advisable. The reason most of us haven't developed a full range of strategies for managing disagreement is that we favor those with which we have the most skill. We hone these skills until they become styles. *Styles* are unconscious or reflexive reactions. In contrast, *strategies* are deliberately selected because we believe they are appropriate to a given situation.

If you want to use a strategy and haven't developed the concomitant interpersonal skills, practice in a low-risk environment first. You might practice your bargaining skills at Sears, or your domination skills by getting a hotel manager to extend your checkout time.

Setting

Mutually decide on a starting and ending time, and a private location that, preferably, is neutral. Rather than either person's office, consider a conference room.

Tone

Set a tone of respect and goodwill to reduce stress.

- Use "I" messages, not "You always . . ."

- Take responsibility for your feelings, rather than blame the other person for how you are feeling.

- Listen *underneath* the other person's words for his or her feelings.

- Listen nondefensively. Don't get preoccupied preparing a rebuttal.

- Allow the other person to complete his or her statements without interruption.

- Pay attention to nonverbal messages that communicate what is *not* being said.

Written Agreements

Many agreements are more effective when committed to writing and provide a helpful reference when memories get hazy.

Where feasible, note points of agreement as the discussion progresses. In your search for specific phrasing, the intentions of both parties will be clarified.

Monitoring

Some agreements are fragile and can unravel. Wherever necessary, decide how results of the agreement will be reviewed.

- What will be measured?

- How?

- By whom?

- For how long?

- What will constitute a successful outcome?

Consequences of Noncompliance

Discuss what happens *if* . . . . A big *if* is the possibility of noncompliance. Whether a legally binding contract or a note taped to the refrigerator door distributing household chores, the consequences of not living up to the agreement should be decided in advance.

Reinforce

Find ways to positively reinforce behavior that supports the agreement.

As we become better able to constructively deal with our differences, the fear of disagreement need no longer be a menacing source of stress in our lives. We move closer to living together in a peaceful, productive world with less tension and anxiety.

Review

> ### *Your Personal Action Options*
> ## MANAGING DISAGREEMENT CONSTRUCTIVELY
>
> When confronting a disagreement:
>
> ### 1. Apply the four guiding principles.
>
> - Maintain mutual respect.
> - Search for common ground.
> - Listen empathically.
> - Let go of having to be right.
>
> Commit the principles to memory.
>
> ### 2. Diagnose the situation.
> Your diagnosis will affect the strategy you select for implementation.
>
> ### 3. Plan a strategy.
> Consciously select one of the nine strategies that best matches your situation. Decide how *flexible* and how *personally involved* you want to be.
>
> ### 4. Implement and follow up.
> Set and maintain a tone of self-respect and mutual dignity.

NOTE: The *Management of Differences Inventory* is available in booklet form to help you identify your current style preferences for managing disagreement. Also available is a feedback edition that enables you to learn how others see you handling disagreement with them. These inventories are available from the Center For Management Effectiveness, P.O. Box 1202, Pacific Palisades, CA 90272, (310) 459-6052.

CHAPTER 12

INNER SOURCES OF STRESS AND STRENGTH

Uncomfortable? Mostly, we look outside ourselves for the source of our discomfort. In this chapter, we will look inside—at hidden sources of stress among our "multitude of contradictory selves." As Pogo observed: "We have met the enemy, and he is us."

Each of us is a unique, never-before-never-again universe existing on many planes of consciousness, many levels of awareness.

Early in life we develop patterns as we attempt to fulfill basic needs for survival, nurturing and acceptance. In time, these response patterns configure into *subpersonalities*.

Artists and writers have long been sensitive to the complex mixture of internalized selves or subpersonalities:

> "There are times when I look over the various parts of my character with perplexity. I recognize that I am made up of several persons and that the person that has the upper hand at the moment will inevitably give place to another."
>
> —Somerset Maugham

> "There are other men in me besides the patient ass who sits here in a tweed jacket."
>
> —D. H. Lawrence

Our inner characters cluster around two poles: ***power*** and ***vulnerability.*** *Power-seeking* subpersonalities include the Pusher, Perfectionist, Judge and Critic; *vulnerable* subpersonalities include the Scared Kid, Hurt Child, Pleaser and Victim. These characters, and others, are the artists of our inner theater. Each member of this all-star cast believes he or she has the leading role, and fights for the limelight.

The script is predictable.

- The Pusher's role is to get you to accomplish more, make endless lists, work harder and longer.

- The Perfectionist wants every detail flawless, never mind the cost to you in time or energy.

- The Critic, who picks you to pieces finding fault is never satisfied with your work.

- The Judge compares your performance with others, using the Perfectionist's standards, and finds you guilty as charged by the Critic.

Subpersonality Defense Systems

While our vulnerable selves feel threatened and under attack by these inner powerhouses, subpersonalities are not intent on destroying us. Rather, their original purpose was to protect our vulnerability in a world where we, as children, were powerless. Often, these defense systems helped us survive.

For our purposes in managing stress, the subpersonality framework offers insight to understand the Type A pattern. Characters in the Pusher-Perfectionist-Judge-Critic constellation compete with one another in a desperate effort to protect the Vulnerable Child who felt overwhelmed early on.

Most Type A behavior starts in childhood as a way to win attention, recognition and approval from parents and other authority figures. Eventually, striving-pushing behavior crystallizes into a pattern we call Type A. When this pattern is practiced compulsively in adult life, it drains energy and increases the risk of illness. Once the Type A subpersonality group takes control, the playful creative child is lost to us, and much of the joy in life goes with it. We assume a too-serious attitude, which throws us off balance and undermines our resilience.

The Inner Critic At Work

The key to moving beyond your Type A pattern is to recognize this cast of "characters" and disidentify from them so they do not control you. They need direction. Your challenge is to develop enough awareness to see where the subpersonalities are destructive and to consciously set limits.

> *Carl is an extremely competent, highly intelligent executive with a history of explosive job endings. Either he quits in indignation or gets fired, in his view, always unfairly. At the peak of his potential, disillusioned by the business world, he abruptly changed careers. When he came to us for stress counseling, he was well on his way to his first heart attack.*
>
> *We guided Carl through an introspective process that helped him discover his self-destructive pattern. He identified an idealistic, fair-minded subpersonality he named Honest John. Honest John is above reproach. He insists on right or wrong with no in-between shades of interpretation. Honest John expects and demands that everyone agree with him. When they don't, he gets furious. He moralizes, preaches and in a storm of self-righteousness quits or gets fired.*
>
> *As the light dawned for Carl, he separated himself from his subpersonality. While he respects Honest John, Carl does not demand that others live by his idealistic expectations. Carl is now able to maintain his integrity in relationships and, to his continuing surprise, finds them easier and more rewarding.*

As adults, the inner stress we feel comes from unconsciously repeating our past in the present. The constant harangue of our inner Pushers and Critics lets us know how we fail to measure up, how much more we should do, and what to do next and next and next. When outside our conscious control, these inner voices push us off balance and destroy our sense of self-worth. They are supported and amplified by our culture that says collectively: "Work hard, play to win, perform in and out of bed, use your head, hide your feelings and do not, under any circumstances, show vulnerability. Don't allow yourself to be seen as weak."

Hal is a talented film director. After a streak of successes, he found himself broke, outside the mainstream, and wondering how he got there. We discovered Hal's Rebel and Hippie subpersonalities left over from the 1960s. They hated the establishment, and when his bosses didn't like his work, these subpersonalities were triggered, saying: "Take your job and shove it."

Word got around that Hal was difficult to work with. Because Hal's Rebel and Hippie subpersonalities did not value his salary, they squandered his hard-earned money on motorcycles and fast cars that Hal frequently wrecked. Once Hal realized who had been running his life, he deliberately began to develop other aspects of his nature. He changed his attitude, brought more respect to his colleagues in the workplace, and started saving for a home.

When we identify totally with any one subpersonality, we lose touch with who we really are. We lose the flexibility needed to respond appropriately to the changing scenarios in our lives. The Workaholic-Pusher-Critic-Perfectionist patterns drive away the Inner Child, who is curious, playful and spontaneous. This particular imbalance is at the root of much inner stress that masquerades as an outer problem.

Reducing stress and harnessing the strength of our inner selves is a lifelong process of healing and empowering yourself. It requires *recognition, disidentification* and *integration*.

Step 1: Recognize Your Subpersonalities

One effective way to recognize your subpersonalities is simply to sense your mood and notice how your body feels. Each subpersonality has a different "feel." When we see a client complaining about his gross failings, the culprit is usually a powerful Critic-Perfectionist. When we see a harried, overscheduled person with long to-do lists on the verge of burnout, the Pusher is often in control. Simply becoming aware of multiple selves leads to greater self-understanding and relieves stress.

The following exercise helps you understand where your dominant inner voices originated.

Exercise 11

Find a comfortable chair and, after reading the following paragraphs, close your eyes. (If feasible, read the exercise into a tape recorder and listen to your own voice as it takes you on a journey to your childhood.)

Become aware of your breathing. Breathe deeply. With each breath, allow yourself to go back in time to when you were a very young child, perhaps three or four years old.

Be that young child lying in your bed. Notice what your room looks like; what you are wearing. You are not able to sleep because you hear your parents' voices. You want to hear what they are saying. You get out of bed, crawl silently to the door of your bedroom, opening it just a crack. Your mother and father (or other important older people in your life) are talking about you. Listen carefully. What are they saying? What do they like and what do they not like about you?

As you feel ready, open your eyes and write what you heard about you. If you heard nothing, imagine what they would say.

_____

_____

_____

_____

_____

_____

_____

_____

_____

_____

Review what you have just written, looking for patterns that are still active in your life. You may be unwittingly perpetuating what you believed your parents thought and felt about you while you were a growing child.

Any unexamined beliefs you inflexibly maintain in adulthood are no longer appropriate. The irony is that they may have been only partially valid even when you embraced them. Your challenge now is to become aware of and examine these embedded beliefs in the light of your thinking today. Are they still relevant? If not, why not choose to let them go?

Step 2: Disidentification

Once you break the illusion that your behavioral patterns are *you*, you can separate your identity from them; you can even appreciate them. From a larger perspective, you can see that you are more than any or all of your inner self-images. Your awareness unlocks the door, freeing you to be yourself. The ability to self-witness is worth developing; it contains the seed of higher consciousness.

Disidentifying is an ongoing process in which your inner witness nonjudgmentally observes your subpersonalities, and sees them as parts, not all of you. The goal of disidentification is twofold:

- To regain your central core, the essence of your being.
- To free the energy locked away in rigid belief systems.

Step 3: Integration

Roberto Assagioli, creator and pioneer of the concept of subpersonalities, describes the need to harmonize disparate or conflicting parts into a unity of the self, working for the good of the whole.

> "At the heart of the self there is both an active and passive element, an agent and a spectator. Self-awareness involves our being a witness—a pure, objective, loving witness—to what is happening within and without. In this sense, the self is not a dynamic element in itself but is a spectator who watches the flow.

> "There is another part of the inner self—the will-er or the directing agent—that actively intervenes to orchestrate the various functions and energies of the personality, to make commitments and to instigate action in the external world.

> "So at the center of the self there is a unity of masculine and feminine, will and love, action and observation."[1]

Subpersonalities are only harmful when they control you. When you get stuck in a fixed pattern of behavior, including Type A, subpersonalities fail to work for the good of the entire organism and symptoms of illness develop.

The key is to develop an inner "aware executive," primarily through daily meditation, who is capable of orchestrating your subpersonalities to harmonize with the energies of your true self.

Additional approaches to learning more about your inner sources of strength and stress are journal writing, dream work and psychotherapy. We recommend the "Voice Dialogue" work of Hal Stone and Sidra Winkleman, particularly their book *Embracing Our Selves* as a means of digging deeper.[2]

Review

Your Personal Action Options
INNER SOURCES OF STRENGTH

1. **Observe your subpersonalities.**
   Notice as they come and go each day. Deep relaxation (see Chapter 14) sets the stage for observing subpersonalities.

2. **Monitor self-criticism.**
   If you have a harsh inner Critic, notice and *write* his (or her) insults about your failings and shortcomings. Examine the validity of these barbs. Replace them with encouraging, supportive, nurturing statements.

CHAPTER 13

LETTING GO

A Zen fable about letting go involves two monks together on a pilgrimage. After many days of silent journey in heavy rain through the mountains, a beautiful woman appeared, about to cross a muddy stream. The elder monk graciously lifted and carried her in his arms safely to the other side.

The monks continued walking without speaking for several days until the second monk, unable to contain himself any longer, blurted, "How could you have picked that woman up? We must not look at a woman, much less touch one!"

After a few moments, the first monk replied gently, "I put her down days ago; I see you are still carrying her."

Letting Go of the Past

Living in the present moment and letting go of the past is a powerful and practical approach to staying healthy and reducing stress. Feelings related to present events give you vital feedback. But if you don't let them go, they will undermine your health. Releasing regret, disappointment, guilt, resentment and blame, all rooted in the past, opens the way for positive new experiences to flow into your life.

Exercise 12

Place a check mark next to each of the following statements that is generally true for you.

- ❏ I often become preoccupied with events during the day and cannot fully relax at home.

- ❏ I still resent experiences that happened long ago.

- ❏ I am holding onto a grudge.

- ❏ I have trouble letting go of people even when it is appropriate to do so.

- ❏ I find it hard to forgive.

If you checked more than one statement, you can benefit from practicing the art of detachment.

Expressing Your Loss

When you suffer the loss of a loved one, a mourning process is natural. You need to give yourself permission and time to feel the pain, and cry about the hurt. Allowing yourself to experience the full range of your grief, including anger and abandonment as well as sorrow, eventually brings release. You will be able to gradually commit yourself to building new relationships, seeking new career opportunities or simply becoming expansive again.

During times of loss, a good friend or counselor can be a comfort. If you are alone, visualize a supportive, loving presence. Express your feelings in whatever ways seem best for you. Writing and painting what you are experiencing often helps. Comfort yourself with the knowledge that you will let go and relax into acceptance in your own time and natural rhythm.

When we lose a well-deserved promotion or prize to a less-deserving person or are betrayed by a trusted partner, we need to feel the injustice, taste the rejection. Then comes the time to detach—before your anger glues you to the past. Remorse and revenge do not serve you well. Old angers can poison our bodies, often finding expression in heart trouble, ulcers, even cancers.

Nursing a grudge or resentment keeps the wound open. You experience stress not just once, but *every time* you recall the event. No matter how justified anger may have been, we continue to carry it at a tremendous physical and emotional cost. We need to forgive others to heal ourselves.

To forgive does not necessarily mean to forget. Its primary purpose is to help you to let go and move on; to get back into a healthy pattern of living. Forgiving opens your heart to joy, love and humor—three of life's greatest medicines. Forgiveness brings harmony and inner peace in place of guilt and resentment.

You do not have to tell anyone you have forgiven them; forgiveness happens within us. Try the following oral forgiveness exercise adapted from Edith Stauffer's *Unconditional Love and Forgiveness*[1] Repeat the exercise as often as needed each time a resentment appears.

Exercise 13

Recall a specific incident that felt hurtful to you, and a person toward whom you feel resentment. Are you willing to stop punishing yourself for the behavior of that person? Ask: "Am I willing to let go?" If so, proceed.

If you are *not willing,* ask yourself how many more weeks, months or years you are willing to suffer. Plan to do this forgiveness exercise at that time. Remind yourself that as long as you hold resentment in your mind and body you are hurting yourself more than anyone else.

Read the following statements aloud, to yourself, completing them appropriately where blank spaces appear.

Step 1
I, _____ , (say your own name) want to stop blaming, punishing and hurting myself for what _____ has said or done. (You may say another's name—or your own name if you are feeling guilt or shame for something you have said or done.)

Step 2
I have been holding onto anger and resentment, self-blame or guilt because _____ . (Describe one incident briefly.)

Step 3
I would have preferred that you had _____ . (With your eyes closed, imagine the person you decided to forgive in front of you. Say the action or words you would have preferred to experience or hear.)

Step 4

However, you did not do that. You did not do or say what I would have preferred. Now I choose to release this incident. I choose to let it go and be free of it.

Step 5

I turn over to you full responsibility for your actions. I have decided to stop suffering and choose to release and heal this incident now.

Step 6

I cancel all expectations, conditions and demands that you, ____(name)____, should be any certain way that I wanted you to be. (This may be a tough step to take. Breathe deeply. Feel yourself let go of all demands.)

Step 7

After you complete steps 1 through 6, close your eyes and go within. Feel the release of letting go and allowing ____(name)____ to take full responsibility for his or her actions. Experience stress leaving your body as you continue breathing deeply.

> *Become aware of your ability to love. Become aware of the compassionate part of you.*

From this wise, loving, compassionate place, send your unconditional acceptance to this person. (This can be a person who is no longer alive.) See the individual in your mind as a worthy and deserving human being. Send peace and forgiveness. To forgive is to let go of what is harming you. Appreciate this gift to yourself.

Take all the time you need to feel this experience. Now scan your body. Are you still holding on, feeling tight anywhere? If so, repeat the process, starting over with Step 1.

The essence of forgiving is captured in the Buddhist "Loving Kindness Meditation."[2]

> *If anyone has hurt or harmed me*
> *knowingly or unknowingly in*
> *thought, word or deed, I freely*
> *forgive them.*
>
> *And I ask forgiveness if I have*
> *hurt anyone or harmed anyone*
> *knowingly or unknowingly in*
> *thought, word or deed.*

Each time you forgive, you release stress. The energy spent hurting yourself by holding onto resentment will become available for expressing creativity and love. Watch your relationships improve.

Letting Go of Negative Expectations

> Every moment is always being born, always new, emerging from that complete unknown which we call the future.[3]
>
> —Alan Watts

Expectation gets in the way of living. Ruminating about what *may* happen is a distraction from what *is* happening.

Letting go of future expectations does not mean abandoning personal visions, goal setting and planning. These activities provide direction to our lives and prepare us to meet contingencies.

Expectations become self-fulfilling prophesies. If we expect the worst to happen, research demonstrates that chances of the worst happening increase.[4]

One executive prided himself on being a good judge of the future performance of recently hired personnel. After his initial encounter with a new employee, he decided whether the individual would succeed or fail. He told other managers so they could score his predictive acumen—indicating who would be "comers" and who would be "turkeys." And sure enough, just as the "self-fulfilling prophecy" hypothesized, he was mostly right.

Much preoccupation with the future is concerned with insecurity. Instead of living, we *prepare to live*. While the dream of *golden years* is enticing, in truth, there are no *golden years,* only golden moments.

Helen Keller counsels:

> "Security is mostly a superstition. It does not exist in nature.
> Life is either a daring adventure or nothing."

Letting Go of Others

Letting go means giving up control. It requires trust in one's own power. The infant has no choice but to cling to its mother's breast. The central task of growing up is to wean ourselves away from dependency. However, even in adulthood many of us still are demanding that a lover, wife, husband, child or guru play a parental role.

When we feel unworthy, we rely on another's love to replace the love we do not feel for ourselves. We come to depend on that person for our sense of self. An example of such a relationship is the man who was questioned about how he liked a movie that he and his companion had seen earlier that day. He replied: "I don't know yet, I haven't had a chance to ask my girlfriend."

To check if you have created one or more dysfunctional relationships, try Exercise 14, adapted from Co-Dependents Anonymous.[5]

Exercise 14

Place a check mark next to each statement that is generally true of your behavior in a specific relationship.

❏ My good feelings about who I am stem from being liked and approved by you.

❏ I am not concerned with how I feel; I am concerned with how you feel. I am not concerned with what I want; I wonder what you want.

❏ I "give" to feel safe in our relationship.

❏ Your personal appearance is important to me because how you look reflects on me.

❏ I value your opinion and way of doing things more than my own.

❏ My fear of your anger or rejection determines what I say and do.

If you checked two or more statements, you may be in an overly-dependent relationship.

Letting go is caring enough about others to let them make their own mistakes, earn their own victories, and take responsibility for their own lives. The bottom line of good stress management in relationships is to accept others exactly as they are and to get clear about one another's boundaries.

The Ultimate Letting Go

No area of stress management is more challenging than how we handle death. Two factors that exacerbate stress are *uncertainty* and *lack of control*. What is more uncertain than how and when each of us will die? What is more beyond our power to control than the inevitability of our own death?

> "Die, die and die—
> and live as a free man."
>
> —old Zen saying

Until we accept death as part of life, we fill space with possessions and time with busyness. Sogyal Rinpoche observes that when people learn they are dying, the realization shakes them into seeing they haven't lived as they wanted. But then it's too late.[6]

To live more fully and relax into your true nature, without the drumroll of a life-threatening illness, you must ask:

- What brings me happiness?

- How can I live my life more fully or deeply?

- What am I contributing?

- What love have I brought into the lives of others?

Living in the Present

When you are fully present, there is no room for anxiety.

Nowhere is living in the *here and now* more compelling than in the sexual experience, where two problems often occur:

- Protecting one's vulnerability

- Having a goal orientation

If you protect yourself by withholding your hurt, anger or resentment, these emotions take up the space for expressing love, caring and appreciation.

If you strive for a sexual goal, you miss the joy of the journey. Once you have a goal, your mind gets into the act; you start to *think* about performing. Thinking destroys spontaneity and takes you away from the direct experience. When sex is linked to *successfully* achieving some objective, the result is bound to be *performance anxiety*. Feeling uptight is not conducive to sexual or any other kind of pleasure. You can be present only when you let go of expectations. When you are fully present, opening yourself to the pleasure of each timeless moment together, then excitement flows and you feel alive and vital.

A vivid character dedicated to living fully in the present is Zorba the Greek. According to Zorba:

> "What's happening today, this minute, that's what I care about. I say: 'What are you doing this moment, Zorba?' 'I'm sleeping.' 'Well, sleep well.' 'What are you doing at this moment, Zorba?' 'I'm working.' 'Well, work well.' 'What are you doing at this moment, Zorba?' 'I'm kissing a woman.' 'Well, kiss her well. And forget all the rest while you are doing it; there's nothing else on earth, only you and her! Get on with it!' "[7]

> This moment is all we have. The past is gone, the future never arrives. When we are preoccupied with the future, we miss living now. By setting aside past memories and future expectations, we create the opportunity, the freedom, to be truly alive. We can enjoy this precious gift of life only one moment at a time.

Review

> ### *Your Personal Action Options*
> ### LETTING GO
>
> **1. Release anger constructively.**
> Acknowledge to yourself what you really do feel, regardless of whether you feel right or wrong about being angry. ("How can I be angry with that poor, helpless person?")
>
> **2. Express anger so that it does not hurt you or the other person.**
> Paint it, dance it, literally run it off. Give yourself permission to write a letter full of four-letter words that you later burn. (Burning is a great metaphor for "releasing.")
>
> **3. Let go, move on.**
> Whenever possible, deal with situations in a way that allows you closure, so that you may open to living fully in the present. Then, as Zorba advises, get on with it.
>
> **4. Meditate daily.**
> Practice being fully present, without expectations or even thoughts. Take time to sense your arms and legs, your belly, your breath.

CHAPTER 14

DEEP RELAXATION

Deep relaxation is a natural way to both resist and recuperate from stress.

The relaxation techniques in this chapter were chosen because we found them easy to learn, enjoyable and highly effective. Each enables you to relax, while training you to focus your attention and improve your concentration.[1]

You already possess the power to reduce tension in your body and anxiety in your life. Your body responds to anxious thoughts with muscle tension, which further increases your subjective experience of anxiety. As you relax deeply, your autonomic nervous system and endocrine system reverse the fight-or-flight response. People who regularly practice some form of relaxation report less tension, more energy, greater self-confidence and less illness.

As you release tension and anxiety, you can better cope with the situation that led to your feeling disturbed. Released muscle tension improves your ability to listen to what is being said, think clearly and act appropriately.

We present three techniques to give you the option of choosing one or more that works well for you. "Deep relaxation" is quite different from ordinary relaxation; it is more than the absence of excessive muscle tension and feeling peaceful. Deep relaxation puts you into an altered state of consciousness, allowing your natural healing life force to take over and restore your mind-body balance.

Progressive Muscle Relaxation

At the first hint of danger, more than 600 muscles that animate the human skeleton contract. During an ordinary day, filled with the usual pressures of living, you repeatedly brace your muscles to prepare for action.

Because *civilized* stress is not released by fight or flight, you hold on to muscle tension and grow accustomed to it. As time goes on, you lose awareness of which muscles are chronically tight. Progressive Muscle Relaxation, Exercise 15, helps you let go and also enables you to recognize which muscles are overly tense. As you practice this exercise over the coming days and weeks, symptoms such as backache, shoulder pain and tension headache are likely to be eased.

We recommend that you carefully read the instructions before starting all relaxation exercises, then put the book aside. You may make your own audiotape of the techniques or purchase one.[2]

Exercise 15

Your active participation is now required. Select a chair that supports your back and sit in a comfortable, more-or-less erect position. Remove or loosen tight clothing, eyeglasses and wristwatch.

- **Begin breathing deeply. . . .**
  As you inhale, first fill the lower section of your lungs by moving your abdomen outward to make room for the air. Next, fill the middle part of your lungs as your lower ribs expand. Finally, fill the upper portion of your lungs by raising your chest slightly. (Allow these three steps to flow in one continuous inhalation.) Hold your breath briefly. Exhale slowly, pulling in abdomen to help your lungs empty. Repeat this process as you take three or four long, deep breaths. Then, breathe normally.

  From this point on, close your eyes so you can become more sensitively aware of the contrasting feelings of taut and relaxed muscles.

- **Focus your attention on your feet. . . .**
  Lift your feet slightly off the floor and point your toes downward, away from your head. Be gentle to avoid cramping. Study the tightness to become aware of tension signals. Let go. Notice how relaxation is different from the tension. Repeat the process and this time, let go just enough to release half the tension and feel what that is like. Now release the tension fully. Rest comfortably for a moment as you feel the pleasant release sensation, and notice the differing sensations of tension and relaxation.

Repeat this procedure of tension and release, followed by tension, half release and full release, with each of the following muscle groups, one at a time:

- Curl your feet and toes back toward your head.

- Tighten your buttocks and thighs, pressing your heels down toward the floor without touching it.

- Tighten your stomach muscles.

- Hold both arms in front of you in a horizontal position, palms down, and spread your fingers wide.

- Keep your arms out and turn them over, palms up. Make fists with both hands and curl them toward your head, keeping your arms in a horizontal position and your fists tightly clenched.

- With both arms still in front of you, relax your fingers and tense your biceps.

- Shrug your shoulders upward toward your ears.

- Gently arch your shoulders back as though you are trying to touch your shoulder blades together.

- Bend your head forward to your chest.

- Turn your head from side to side as far as it will go, first in one direction, later in the other.

- Raise your eyebrows. Wrinkle your forehead by frowning.

- Make your facial muscles taut by grimacing ("screwing up" your face) with your eyelids tightly closed.

- Open your mouth and eyes wide. Stick your tongue out as far as possible and make a deep growling sound.

- Yawn and stretch all over.

Scan your body for residual tightness anywhere. Tighten and then let the tension dissolve from any area that is not relaxed. As you end with a minute or two of deep breathing, feel the calm and give yourself a positive suggestion to become alert. Tell yourself, "I am wide awake, fully present, and feeling great," as you prepare to return to your regular activities.

Progressive Muscle Relaxation may be practiced on a regular schedule or whenever you feel anxious or tense.

Meditative Relaxation

A "meditative mood" is commonly experienced while listening to the rhythmic sound of the surf or watching the glow of a campfire's embers. These spontaneous forms of altered consciousness are similar to but not the same as those elicited by an intentional meditation exercise.

A regular program of Meditative Relaxation, from 15 to 20 minutes daily, releases accumulated stress. Harvard Medical School's Herbert Benson writes: "Meditative techniques cause scientifically measurable changes: metabolism, heart and respiration rates decrease; alpha wave output (brain waves associated with feelings of well-being) intensifies; and a general calming effect ensues."[3]

When this technique is practiced regularly, it improves health and concentration.

Exercise 16

Sit in a straight-backed chair or on cushions, keeping your back comfortably straight.

Step 1
Release muscle tension.

You may use Progressive Muscle Relaxation (Exercise 15) or the following tension-release alternative. With your eyes closed, become aware of your feet and release any tightness you may sense. Be aware of your breathing without altering its rhythm. As you inhale, imagine your breath as a refreshing stream of air that bathes over your feet, soothing them. Imagine your breath picking up released tension from your feet and sweeping it out of your body as you exhale.

Within one or two more cycles of breathing, all tightness will melt from your feet. As it does, focus on the next body area in the order indicated below, repeating this method: release tension, breathe relaxation into the area, exhale all tightness.

- Calves
- Thighs
- Buttocks and genital area
- Hands
- Forearms and upper arms
- Abdomen and chest

- Lower and middle back

- Shoulders and neck

- Mouth, face and scalp

Step 2
Focus your attention on your breathing while maintaining a passive attitude.

Keep your eyes closed as you complete the process of releasing muscle tightness. Each time you *exhale*, silently count a number, starting with *one*. Breathe in normally through your nose and, as you breathe out through your slightly open mouth, count *two* silently as you exhale. Repeat this procedure until you reach *four*, then start the cycle over, counting *one* on your next exhalation.

During this meditative process, as thoughts enter your mind, notice them, let them go, and gently return your attention to breathing and counting. Do the same with outside noises, noticing the sounds, letting them go and returning to your silent counting and breathing. If you feel an itch or your clothes feel tight, scratch yourself or loosen your clothing so you feel comfortable.

Variations:

- You may replace the counting with an *affirming word or phrase* that has meaning for you, such as *peace, joy dwells within* or *divine love.*

- Another option is wordless. As you breathe in, focus on the expansion of your abdomen. As you exhale, focus on its contraction.

Step 3
Just be.

After 15 to 20 minutes of relaxed breathing and counting, sit quietly for as long as you wish. Allow your sense of peace to permeate throughout your body, nourishing each cell. This is a wonderful time to appreciate the unity of life. If you are so inclined, imagine your feelings of well-being radiating out to the world.

Autogenic Training

The Autogenic Training form of letting go is particularly useful for getting to sleep or falling back to sleep. If you have had a frenetic day or feel keyed up, this form of relaxation prepares you for sleep. A common cause of sleeplessness is preoccupation with what has happened during the day or with what you fear will be a problem tomorrow.

Autogenic (self-generated) Training breaks the preoccupation-worry loop, using a series of phrases that you repeat to yourself. These phrases act as all-clear signals to the unconscious mind, which then manifests relaxation in the body. As with meditation, the key to this process is to surrender all effort to make something happen. Effort inhibits the process; letting go promotes deep relaxation. Let the pleasant sensations of relaxation come over you without striving for them.

After reviewing the instructions, proceed with your eyes closed.

Exercise 17

You may either use a chair or, if you want to overcome sleeplessness, lie in bed on your back. Prepare yourself by taking a few deep breaths, exhaling fully. If thoughts occur to you during the process, observe them and let them go.

Release muscle tension using either Exercise 15, Progressive Muscle Relaxation, or Exercise 16, Step 1.

Focus on your right hand and repeat silently to yourself three or four times: "My right hand is heavy." Pause briefly between repetitions. Say the phrase at a pace that feels comfortable to you. Each time you repeat this phrase, allow the sensation of heaviness to move effortlessly into your right hand. Do not be concerned about whether or not your right hand actually feels heavy. Say to yourself: "It really doesn't matter (if my right hand feels heavy or not".)

Next, shift your focus from your hand to your "self" as you repeat: "I am calm and serene. I am at peace." As you repeat these phrases three or so times, allow yourself to experience calmness and serenity. You may want to visualize yourself in a peaceful setting in nature—in a meadow, at the beach, near a brook.

Shift the focus to your left hand and repeat the process.

Follow this procedure with any or all of the following phrases. In other words, after each body statement, repeat: "I am calm and serene. I am at peace." If you want to fall asleep, you are likely to do so before you have completed the following phrase list:

1. My right hand is heavy.
My left hand is heavy.
My right hand and arm are heavy.
My left hand and arm are heavy.
My hands and arms are heavy,
and it really doesn't matter.

2. My right foot is heavy.
My left foot is heavy.
My right foot and leg are heavy.
My left foot and leg are heavy.
My feet and legs are heavy,
and it really doesn't matter.

3. My right hand is warm.
My left hand is warm.
My right hand and arm are warm.
My left hand and arm are warm.
My hands and arms are warm,
and it really doesn't matter.

4. My right foot is warm.
My left foot is warm.
My right foot and leg are warm.
My left foot and leg are warm.
My feet and legs are warm,
and it really doesn't matter.

5. My arms and legs are heavy.
My arms and legs are warm.
My arms and legs are heavy and warm.
My heartbeat is calm and regular,
and it really doesn't matter.

6. My arms and legs are heavy and warm.
My heartbeat is calm and regular.
My breathing is relaxed and comfortable,
and it really doesn't matter.

7. My arms and legs are heavy and warm.
My heartbeat is calm and regular.
My breathing is relaxed and comfortable.
My solar plexus is heavy and warm,
and it really doesn't matter.

8. My arms and legs are heavy and warm.
My heartbeat is calm and regular.
My breathing is relaxed and comfortable.
My solar plexus is heavy and warm,
My forehead is cool,
and it really doesn't matter.

Proceed slowly at first, with 15-to-20-minute practice sessions each day, focusing on one set of phrases. Take a week to allow your body to feel comfortable with the phrases. Once your body responds to your suggestions, you can do an Autogenic session during a brief break, sitting at your office desk.

When you start, limit the number of phrase sets to what feels comfortable. Each week or so, you may add to your routine. Autogenic Training can be used either to facilitate getting to sleep or in place of Meditative Relaxation. Unless your intention is sleep, end each session with, "I feel relaxed, refreshed and alert."

General Deep Relaxation Instructions

Your ability to let go of accumulated daily tension will be assisted by designing your lifestyle to include at least one relaxation exercise. Most of your day is devoted to **doing;** this is a chance to add balance to your life by just **being.** After all, we are human beings, not human doings. If you select a morning time for deep relaxation, it may energize your day. Or, after returning home in the evening, deep relaxation helps you unwind and provides a welcome transition between work and free time.

For a quick calming effect, whenever you need it, use deep diaphragmatic breathing. As you breathe in, allow your abdomen to expand, then your rib cage and chest. Exhale slowly as you gently pull in your stomach to expel the last of the stale air.

Select the same pleasant location for your relaxation exercise each day, if feasible. Unplug telephones and discourage intrusions. You may invite others to join you; communication afterward often improves.

Once you learn to relax deeply during your daily practice sessions, you will have a new portable skill. You will be able to respond differently to events that otherwise would have generated stress. Now when you become aware of a stress cue (in your body, feelings or actions) you can remind yourself to initiate the deep relaxation response. You will be in charge of how you respond. In conjunction with a personally meaningful spiritual orientation, meditation helps reestablish inner balance and harmony.

Review

Your Personal Action Options

DEEP RELAXATION

1. **Take a relaxation break every day.**
   Master at least one deep relaxation technique and use it daily to create balance between activity and rest.

2. **Get a massage.**
   Massage is a wonderful reward that is not fattening and only mildly addictive.

CHAPTER 15

REACHING OUT

In connecting, we help one another cope with stress by buffering the impact of crisis and change. Our social networks provide

► **Emotional Support**
   Friends who share a bond of caring, trust, empathy and appreciation

► **Practical Support**
   Giving and receiving physical energy, equipment, money, things, information or a fresh perspective

To harvest these benefits, cultivate a social network of people with whom you have various kinds of give-and-take relationships. Like growing a garden, tending your network takes time, care and patience. You may also need to weed occasionally and prune relationships that have become more stressful than helpful.

Your Current Support Network

Most networks grow without intentional design. However you may have assembled yours, it is a good idea to review all the people in your orbit and their relationship to you. In her book, *Necessary Losses,* Judith Viorst says we have "convenience friends, historical friends, crossroads and cross-generational friends, and friends that come when you call at two in the morning."[1] Seeing these relationships visually can help you more consciously create your personal, social and professional network.

Exercise 18

You relate to people in your network at various levels of intimacy. Using the categories we have designated, write the names of people with whom you currently relate. As you fill in the names, appreciate the different levels and worlds in your relationship universe.

Start with people closest to you and write each name one time only (in the *most intimate* applicable level). For example, if Jennifer fits into Companions and also has a formal Role Relationship with you, place Jennifer's name in the Companion Circle.

INTIMATE CIRCLE   NAME

This group is your "inner circle,"
which may include spouse, parents,
siblings, friends. These are the
people in whom you confide and
with whom you confer about
important concerns.

COMPANION CIRCLE   NAME

People in this category are friends
and associates with whom you have
ongoing relationships, but in whom
you would not confide nor call on
in time of need. Thoughts and
feelings are shared within limits that
are mutually comfortable.

ROLE RELATIONSHIP CIRCLE   NAME

These people remain in your life
because of their roles—such as
in-laws, bosses, co-workers,
neighbors and car poolers. You
exchange small favors and maintain
emotional distance with these
people.

Write the name of each person on your list in the appropriate circles.

Draw a line between "ME," at the center of your social support network, and each name in the various circles. Vary the thickness of the line to reflect the quality of support you currently experience in each of these relationships. The thicker the line, the greater the support.

My Current Support Group

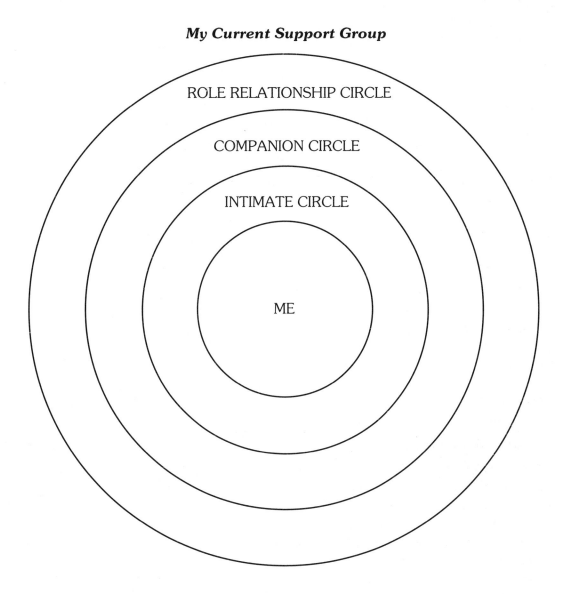

The diagram you completed is the beginning of consciously creating a social network, one that truly serves who you are and what you want to become. Next, ask yourself:

- Do I have enough people in my life who care for and support me?

- Am I spreading myself too thin?

- Are people I depend on there for me when I need them?

- Do I ask for help when appropriate?

- Are my relationships one-sided or mutual?

If you have only one person in your Intimate Circle, are you putting too much pressure on that relationship? Are you too vulnerable to the possible loss of this person? Do you have people to call when you need someone to listen to a confidential problem you are having with an employee? Who would you call if you needed the name of a good doctor or an appropriate computer program?

As La Rochefoucauld observed: "A friend is the most precious of all possessions, and the one we take the least thought about acquiring." Your network is a powerful resource, well worth developing thoughtfully.

Obstacles to Building a Support Network

- **Fear of exposing yourself as weak**
  "If I ask for help, my requests may be interpreted by others as a sign that I am overly dependent."

- **Fear of exposing your vulnerability**
  "If I share my deepest thoughts and feelings, I may appear inadequate or foolish."

- **Fear of closeness and commitment**
  "If I encourage closer relationships, I may be getting myself too deeply involved and too obligated."

- **Fear of rejection**
  "If I stick my neck out to make a friend, I may get turned down or let down. If I ask one person and not others, they may feel that I'm rejecting them."

- **Fear of imposing**
  "Some people may say they are willing to connect, when they really want to say no."

No man is an island entire of itself;
every man is a part of the continent.

—John Donne

Building Relationship Bridges

Some people know how to make allies very well, but not how to get close to people. Here are some ideas.

► **Trust**
The bottom line for a friendship is trust. Relationships falter when trust is betrayed. This applies whether it is a breach of confidentiality at work or a secret affair in a committed relationship. The only trust-building strategy that works is to maintain your integrity, speak your truth, honor your agreements, respect boundaries and, above all, be trustworthy.

► **Risk**
Mutually supportive relationships start when one person reaches out and takes a risk. This may be a small risk, such as choosing to see more often someone you already know at work, joining a group, taking a class, or not depending on your spouse to be your social director.

► **Persevere**
As with anything you want to grow, relationships require attention. What better way to spend time than sharing your mind and heart with someone you enjoy and respect?

Review

> ### *Your Personal Action Options*
> ### REACHING OUT
>
> **1. Cultivate your social network.**
> The *social disease* that lowers the body's resistance is a lack of close friends. Candid, confiding relationships strengthen the body's immune system.
>
> **2. Open your heart to love and friendship.**
> Expand your circle. Let more people touch your heart.

CHAPTER 16

HONORING YOUR BODY

You have been blessed with a brilliantly engineered, magnificently architected home on earth—your body. This amazing piece of *equipment,* with thousands of moving parts and complex interactions, is designed to last a lifetime. With proper care, your body may function continuously to old age using original components. However, your personal action plan must satisfy three basic needs: **regular exercise, good nutrition** and **adequate rest.**

Physical Movement

> The best gift you can give your body is to move it.

What would you give for a prescription so powerful it can bring down elevated blood pressure and cholesterol, melt off unwanted pounds, normalize blood sugar, strengthen bones, increase joint flexibility, tone muscles, promote endurance and improve the quality of sleep? This prescription is so safe that moderate doses cause few if any side effects, and so inexpensive that anyone can afford it.

The wonder medicine is exercise! Our primitive ancestors were hunters and gatherers who moved their bodies up to 15 hours a day. How many hours a day do you move? In our information-driven, computer-run society, most people are physically underactive, and mentally/emotionally overactive, creating an imbalanced mind-body system.

Here are five steps to help you reap the greatest rewards from a physical exercise program:

Step 1
Check your physical condition.

If you are relatively sedentary, arterial narrowing may be occurring. Therefore, before you start a vigorous exercise program, get a medical checkup. Always check out any unusual symptoms with your physician.

Information about the exercise intensity appropriate for your current fitness level lets you determine the best pace for getting enough oxygen to your muscles without threatening your heart's ability to deliver it.

Step 2
Select exercises you enjoy.

Choose physical activities that you can comfortably integrate into your daily life and easily sustain. Anything that gets you moving, which *you* consider fun, will do. Brisk walking, dancing, jogging, cycling indoors or out, skating or swimming laps can fit into a busy schedule.

Step 3
Warm up before and cool down after exercise.

Stretching is an enjoyable way to prepare for movement. The object of limbering is to improve muscle and joint flexibility and prevent injury. When you stretch before and after exercise, hold mild tension for at least ten seconds and relax as you hold the stretch. You may increase your stretch gradually, but avoid going to your limit and don't bounce.[1]

Step 4
Exercise.

If you are relatively inactive, walking is the most natural way to start your exercise program. Walking reduces anxiety, and the relaxing effect lasts for hours. To exercise aerobically, you need to exert yourself enough to reach 85 percent of your heart's maximum rate for 15 to 20 minutes at least every other day.

See the chart below to find your aerobic pulse rate.

Maximum Recommended Pulse Rates for Aerobic Exercise

Age	Pulse Rate	Age	Pulse Rate
20–24	160	45–49	141
25–29	158	50–54	137
30–34	154	55–59	132
35–39	149	60–64	125
40–44	145	65–69	120

Using the chart as a guide, briefly stop exercising after five minutes and take your pulse either at the wrist or neck. Count for ten seconds and multiply by six. While exercising, you should be breathing heavily but still be able to carry on a conversation. Stop any exercise that causes you pain.

Step 5
Reinforce your commitment to regular exercise.

Focus on the benefits. Visualize yourself looking fit and trim, feeling healthy and energized.

Nutrition

Eating is a national pastime. A great difference exists between eating to please your palate and eating to nourish your body. Food has many non-nutritional meanings: success, love, self-indulgence, protection, comfort, a means of control. Recent reactions from clients to their issues with food:

► "I like rich food. All my life I wanted to be able to afford the most expensive restaurants. I moved to the west side of town so I could have any food I wanted whenever I wanted to eat. Now that I'm 50, when we go to a restaurant, my wife says, 'Don't use salt. You can't have dessert. Don't you dare eat red meat.' Anything that tastes good is bad for me."

► "I'm not a compulsive overeater, it's just that once I get started, I can't stop."

► "I'm happy to tell you my middle-of-the-night eating problem is solved. My wife chains my left arm to our headboard at bedtime with just enough length to get me to the bathroom, but not enough to reach the kitchen."

Because so many diets are promoted as healthful, it is easy to be confused. We have selected the most significant and least controversial guidelines from nutritional research.

> One caveat: When in doubt, listen to your body. If any food disagrees with you—gives you gas, cramps, heartburn or an allergic reaction—do not eat that food or combination of foods.

Complex Carbohydrates

Fresh vegetables, fruits, lentils, nuts, seeds, whole grains and cereals should make up 60 to 70 percent of your total calories. Select local produce when available; remove pesticides and preservative waxes by washing or peeling. In addition to vitamins and minerals, these foods provide fiber, the natural laxative that reduces the risk of colon cancer.

Protein Foods

Fish, poultry, lean meat, eggs, dairy products and beans should make up 10 to 20 percent of your total calories. Remove skin from chicken; eat egg yolks in moderation; and use low-fat or nonfat milk and cheeses to reduce cholesterol intake. Watch for allergic reactions to milk and milk products (common to adults except those of Northern European ancestry).

Fats

Only 10 to 20 percent of your total caloric intake each day should be fats. To reverse heart disease, Dean Ornish recommends keeping fat below 10 percent.[2] To calculate your fat intake percentage, start with the food label. Multiply the grams of fat by 9 to get the number of calories derived purely from fat. Then divide the calories from fat by the total calories. For example, a package of processed meat might contain 6 grams of fat. Multiply 6 grams × 9 = 54 calories from fat. If the total calories are 100, then your caloric intake from this food is 54 percent. To further reduce the risk of clogged arteries, breast and colon cancer, balance high-fat with low-fat foods and choose polyunsaturated fats over fats laden with cholesterol.

Food Hazards to Avoid

Avoid processed foods and eat selectively in fast-food restaurants.

Avoid Sugar

Since the first beet-sugar refinery was built in France in 1801, annual per capita consumption has climbed to more than one hundred pounds in every developed nation, with England in the lead. Sugar, honey and molasses all promote tooth decay, higher triglyceride levels, and obesity. These foods have no nutritional value. Even worse, sugar is quickly absorbed into the blood, which the body interprets as a stress sign and prepares to fight or flee. This "sugar rush" throws your system out of balance as the pancreas burns up excess sugar with its insulin. In turn, the liver responds with more sugar plus very low-density lipoproteins which are associated with coronary heart disease. The body is pushed onto a sugar-insulin roller coaster: a burst of energy, then "sugar blues" irritability, followed by insistent hunger pangs demanding more sweets.

What You Can Do

Fresh fruit, yams and other complex carbohydrates take longer to get into the blood stream, and are a superior nutritional source of quick energy. Watch food labels for sugar synonyms, and don't be fooled by ingredients called sucrose, corn sweetener and dextrose. Replace soft drinks with mineral water and fresh diluted juices.

Avoid Caffeine

Caffeine generates stress by stimulating the adrenal glands. Anything beyond two cups of coffee in an eight-hour period can trigger a stress reaction. High blood pressure, insomnia, heart palpitation, tremors, irritability and anxiety are common problems that can be exacerbated by excess caffeine.

What You Can Do

Consider steam-processed decaffeinated coffee, herbal teas and broth. A brisk ten-minute walk improves mental alertness and productivity more effectively than a cup of coffee, without the side effects of "coffee jitters."

Avoid Salt

No biological need exists for high levels of salt. An intake of twelve or more grams of salt a day contributes to elevated blood pressure. An international study with 10,000 participants from 32 countries showed that low salt intake, under three grams a day, correlated significantly with low incidence of hypertension.[3]

What You Can Do

By gradually reducing salt intake, your palate will become more sensitive to the subtle nuances of food tastes. Leave the salt shaker out of your cooking and off your table. Discover the rich variety of herbs, spices and salt-free condiments.

Avoid Fats

Heart attacks, and certain types of breast tumors increase as the amount of saturated fat and cholesterol in the diet increase.

What You Can Do
Reduce to a minimum your consumption of red meats, hard cheeses, whole milk, ice cream, butter, egg yolk and coconut and palm oils. Switch to polyunsaturated vegetable and olive oils that have not been hydrogenated (adding hydrogen saturates the fat). Sauté instead of frying using no more than a tablespoon of oil in a nonstick pan, adding water, broth, or wine if the pan becomes dry.

If Weight Is a Concern

Weight-loss diets do not work for most people in the long run mainly because they involve controlling rather than trusting your body. What *does* work is eating with awareness.

- At the start of each meal, sit comfortably and take two or three deep breaths to help you relax.
- A moment of silence and giving thanks is a lovely way to prepare your body to receive.
- As you eat slowly with awareness take small bites.
- When your body is done it will tell you to stop.

It is comforting to know that just as your body can be trusted to signal stress, it can be trusted to tell you when to eat and how much to eat. Learn to distinguish between hunger pangs and taste-bud appetite. Trusting your body starts by paying attention to its signals.

Begin by making changes you can live with, however small. Take it in stages. Allow each new set of eating behaviors to stabilize before starting the next. Take heart—eating wisely and well is getting easier. Many health-based cookbooks are coming out *every* year, and wholesome cooking as well as gourmet-style *nouvelle cuisine* is catching on in restaurants.[4]

Sleep

A good night's sleep is essential to overall good health and performance. Sleep deprivation can cause irritability, hypersensitivity to criticism and short-term memory loss. Much of the difficulty of insomnia is stress-related—pressure, overwork, holding on to hurts, fears and resentments. If wakefulness is a chronic problem or is accompanied by pain, sweating or difficulty breathing, get a medical evaluation.

Techniques that work for stress-related sleep disorders:

▶ **Eating lightly**

Avoid heavy or hard-to-digest evening meals.

▶ **Walking**

An evening walk helps release the day's concerns. Avoid heavy exercise shortly before bedtime.

▶ **Minimizing stimulation**

To have a restful sleep, avoid watching disturbing television shows during the late evening. Keep task reminders such as unpaid bills out of sight. Avoid caffeinated drinks; try herb teas. Simply holding the warm cup in your hands and watching the steam rise can be soothing.

▶ **Writing for release**

If you are mulling over upcoming events, write about your feelings. Getting them on paper may get them off your mind.

▶ **Autogenic Training**

Experiments show that sleeplessness is associated with an activated autonomic nervous system. A body that tosses and turns is better prepared to dodge rush-hour traffic than to get a restful night's sleep. The Autogenic Training technique presented in Chapter 14 is a natural and potent sleep aid. As tightness, agitation and anxiety fall away, you can help the process along by repeating: "I am relaxing deeper and deeper. I am moving deeper and deeper into restful, peaceful sleep."

▶ **Massage**

The gentle touch of caring hands feels wonderful to everyone who lets go and allows themselves to simply *be* with the experience. Massaging releases nervous tension, aches and fatigue. It switches our bodies from fight-or-flight (sympathetic) mode to rest-digest-heal (parasympathetic) mode and allows our minds to relax.

► **Foot baths**

Just before retiring, sit at the edge of your tub and place your feet in a warm bath. As you let the water swirl down the drain, imagine all your cares also draining away.

► **Avoid sedation**

Minimize the use of sedatives because they interfere with a restful, refreshing sleep—and the natural process of dreaming.

► **Dreams**

The body releases much of the day's tension while we sleep and dream. Disturbing dreams often contain clues about stress that call for attention. An unhappy stockbroker dreams she is suffocating under tons of ticker tape. A frustrated chemist sees his flasks and beakers turn into snakes and dragons. One person had a recurring dream of being in a parade, but always out of step. When she realized how significantly her job schedule violated her natural rhythm, she started doing free-lance work and was able to enjoy restful sleep.

Review

> *Your Personal Action Options*
> **HONORING YOUR BODY**
>
> 1. **Integrate enjoyable movement into your lifestyle.**
>   List physical activities you enjoy and can easily make part of your daily routine. Walk at lunchtime or in the evening, to strengthen your heart, sleep better and create time for relationships. Follow cardiologist Paul Dudley White's counsel: "Walk your dog every day, whether you have a dog or not."
>
> 2. **Expand the variety of fresh foods you eat.**
>   Experiment with nutritious dishes such as whole grain pasta tossed with steamed vegetables, fresh herbs, and sunflower seeds. Try spiking fruit with lemon instead of cream and sugar. Explore different salads, soups and casseroles.

PART FIVE

INTEGRATING STRESS MANAGEMENT

"Whatever you can do,

or dream you can, begin it.

Boldness has genius,

power and magic in it."

—Goethe

CHAPTER 17

YOUR PERSONAL ACTION PLAN

Less Is More

The essence of good stress management is good time management. Time is not money; it's a lot more valuable. Time is your *life*. Time management boils down to two strategies: Work smarter; do less.

Working smarter utilizes technology effectively. The time-saving professional or manager works toward a common, clearly articulated vision, maintains priority boundaries, consolidates and delegates tasks, reduces clutter, minimizes unnecessary interruptions, writes a daily time plan and communicates explicit expectations.

Doing less is the greatest challenge of time and stress management. Gain the clarity to know when to say no to the many activities that distract you from your vision, and the courage to say yes to the few things that really matter. Leave space for unexpected possibilities to present themselves.

Our Perfectionist subpersonality loves to remind us: "Anything worth doing is worth doing well." Rather than be pressured by this inner voice, ask yourself: "What would happen if this weren't done perfectly? What if I didn't do it at all?"

Take time now to review the action options at the end of each chapter.

As you prepare to draft your personal action plan, what few vital areas of your life do you want to further cultivate? What trivial or unrewarding activities do you want to prune? Use the four basic categories—physical, mental, emotional and spiritual—to organize your plan, keeping *lifelong balance* as your central focus. Aim to balance a challenging career with a nurturing home life; excitement and adventure with quiet time for inner reflection.

Articulating the specifics of your plan in writing is helpful. Use the following form to gather and refine your thoughts.

In-Process Action Plan

Desired Changes

Physical

_____

_____

_____

_____

Mental

_____

_____

_____

_____

Emotional

_____

_____

_____

_____

Spiritual

_____

_____

_____

_____

Managing stress is about making choices. Empower yourself by making wise decisions that support your growth and fulfillment.

- Give yourself permission to find and pursue your deepest vision.
- Give yourself the freedom to go for it.
- Listen to your inner voices that urge you toward your vision.
- Select a vision that fits comfortably with your lifestyle.

If you choose *only one* action option that makes your life better, you will have taken an important step. You may initiate other changes as you feel ready.

Once you have completed the design for your personal action plan, we urge you to make a commitment. This pledge is the bridge that connects your vision to full realization.

Commitment to Myself

I take responsibility for improving the quality of my life. I promise to persevere in this endeavor, to honor and take good care of myself. I agree to support the following vision for myself:

_____

_____

_____

I will pursue my vision via these specific activities:

	Starting Date	**Review Date**
1. _____	_____	_____
_____	_____	_____
2. _____	_____	_____
_____	_____	_____
3. _____	_____	_____
_____	_____	_____
4. _____	_____	_____
_____	_____	_____

Your Signature _____

Date _____

Here is how four people translated their scores on the Chapter 5 *Personal Stress Assessment Inventory* into action plans.

▶ **JANET,** age 34 and single, is an executive with a multinational corporation. She is ambitious and invariably takes work home evenings and weekends. Her *Personal Stress Assessment Inventory* Type A "Predisposition" score was 8.6, which is high. Her "Resilience" score, at 62, indicates that she neglects nurturing, self-restorative activities. Job pressures are demanding, and Janet's company is undergoing a major reorganization. If Janet continues her current course, she is a candidate for illness or burnout. She is showing signs of extreme fatigue and depression.

Janet's Personal Action Plan

- Cut down caffeine and sugar to avoid highs followed by feeling drained.

- Pay close attention to body signals for rest. Don't wait until the point of exhaustion.

- Create a more balanced lifestyle. Spend more time with friends. Include outdoor exercise.

- Take time for meals. Eat light lunches, and walk afterward with colleagues to network and revitalize energy.

▶ **PHIL** is a brilliant young doctor with a growing practice. He recently purchased a home and is loaded with professional and personal debts. Phil has no time for anything but his career. He often feels exhausted and has lost his zest for living. By the time he arrives home each evening, he has little left to give. His marriage is no longer a source of comfort. His score for "Continuing Work-Related Stress Sources" is 170, with 110 for "Continuing Personal Stress Sources." Both are excessive.

Phil's Personal Action Plan

- Spend 15 to 30 minutes each day alone, dreaming, writing and planning about my personal vision.

- Devote *quality time* to family. Invite my wife for a romantic date once a week.

- Reduce financial obligations. Cut back office overhead. Find another doctor to share facilities and staff.

► **MIKE,** an architect in his forties is in mid-life crisis. He is married with three school-age children. Despite long hours at work, Mike was passed over for a promotion awarded to a younger associate. Perhaps to prop up his sagging self-confidence, he had a brief extramarital affair. Now he feels guilty at home, trapped in his job and generally moody. His "Resilience" score is 68, and he scored 15 points higher on "Continuing Sources of Stress" he perceives beyond his control versus those within his control. Both Mike and his wife Mary are 20 pounds overweight.

Mike's Personal Action Plan

- Seek professional counsel to address and sort out current issues.

- Use affirmations daily, such as: "I am a worthy person; I don't have to prove my self-worth to anyone."

- Start losing weight. Try out a support group such as Overeaters Anonymous or Weight Watchers. Reduce red meat and desserts; limit alcohol to two glasses of wine, weekends only.

- Plan more adventure, starting with a ski trip with Mary.

► **KAREN,** fiftyish, recently divorced, has two teenagers who are experimenting with drugs. Karen's aging parents are increasingly depending on her for financial and personal support. Living on a secretary's salary since her husband left, Karen must decide if she can afford to stay in her home. Her "Periodic Stress Sources" score is way up at 170. She has trouble sleeping, worries obsessively and feels out of control. Her "Physical Symptoms score" is 20; her "Psychological Symptoms score" is 31. Both reflect pressures she is experiencing. Karen is determined to stop feeling sorry for herself and to make her life work.

Karen's Personal Action Plan

- Get a complete medical checkup. Talk with the doctor about high-stress symptoms.

- Join a self-help group, for emotional support and insights from others with similar concerns.

- Seek a new vision that will focus more on areas of control—such as setting boundaries and limits for her daughters, and deciding what she can and is willing to do for her parents.

- Keep a daily journal and meditate. Stay focused in the present rather than dwelling on regrets about the past or worries about the future.

Freeing and empowering yourself doesn't happen overnight. Like all growth, it is a process that develops over time. Weeks or months of perseverance are required to establish new behavior patterns. With gentle persistence over time, they will gradually become part of your everyday living. As you become clearer about choices that move you closer to realizing your vision, your powers of discrimination will increase. Why not start now?

> If I am not for myself,
>   who will be for me?
> If I am only for myself,
>   what am I?
> If not now, when?
>
> —Hillel, *Wisdom of Our Fathers*

May you realize the vision in your heart as you find balance, joy and peace.

```
┌─────────────────┐
│                 │
│     NOTES       │
│                 │
└─────────────────┘
```

Chapter 1: What This Program Can Do for You

1. C. Weiman, "A Study of Occupational Stressors and the Incidence of Disease," *Journal of Occupational Medicine*, 1977, pp. 119–122.

2. Research on stress and the immune system is discussed in "Neuroendocrine Measures of Stress," by W. McKinnen, A. Baum and P. Morokoff in *Social Psychophysiology and Emotion*, New York: Wiley, 1988, pp. 56–58.

Chapter 3: The Big Picture: Using a Cybernetic Systems Map

1. N. Weiner, *Cybernetics*, New York: Wiley, 1948.

2. S. Suzuki, *Nurtured By Love*, 2nd edition, Smithtown, New York: Exposition-Banner, 1983.

Chapter 5: The Stress Test

1. The scales in this chapter are taken from the PERSONAL STRESS ASSESSMENT INVENTORY™, which is available to the public in booklet form. Write the Center For Management Effectiveness, P.O. Box 1202, Pacific Palisades, CA 90272.

Research on the scales' reliability and validity appear in *Employee Counseling Today*, "Motivating Participation in Stress Management

Training Programs Using A Self-Diagnostic Inventory," D. A. Schorr and H. S. Kindler, Fall 1991; and *Management Communication Quarterly*, "A Review of Instrumentation on Stress," C. W. Downs, G. Driskill and D. Wuthnow, August 1990, pp. 100–126.

Chapter 6: Understanding Your Stress Scores

1. M. Friedman and D. Ulmer, *Treating Type A Behavior and Your Heart*, New York: Knopf, 1984, p. 203.

2. E. Glogow, "Burnout and Locus Control," *Public Personnel Management*, Volume 15, 1986, pp. 79–83.

3. A. Pines and E. Aronson, *Career Burnout*, New York: Free Press, 1988, p. 35.

4. O. C. Simonton and S. Matthews-Simonton, *Getting Well Again*, Los Angeles: Tarcher, 1978.

5. G. E. Schwartz, R. J. Davidson and Daniel Goleman, "Patterning of Cognitive and Somatic Processes in the Self-Regulation of Anxiety: Effects of Meditation Versus Exercise," *Psychosomatic Medicine*, Volume 40, 1978, pp. 321–328.

Chapter 7: Overcoming Type A Predisposition

1. R. Williams, *The Trusting Heart*, New York: *Times* Books, 1989.

2. L. Wright, "The Type A Behavior Pattern and Coronary Artery Disease," *American Psychologist*, Volume 43, 1988, pp. 2–14.

3. M. Friedman and R. H. Rosenman, *Type A Behavior and Your Heart*, New York: Fawcett Crest, 1974.

Chapter 8: Building Resilience

1. Piaget is quoted by T. Lidz in *The Person: His Development Throughout The Life Cycle*, New York: Basic Books, 1968.

2. I. Progoff, *At A Journal Workshop*, New York: Dialogue House, 1975, p. 296.

Chapter 9: Dealing with Life Changes

1. I. Janis and L. Mann, *Decision Making*, New York: Free Press, 1977, p. 155.

Chapter 10: Handling the Daily Grind

1. S. I. Hayakawa, *Symbol, Status and Personality*, New York: Harcourt, Brace and World, 1953.

2. H. S. Kindler, "Two Planning Strategies: Incremental and Transformational Change," *Group & Organization Studies*, Volume 4, 1979, pp. 476–484.

Chapter 11: Managing Disagreement Constructively

1. H. S. Kindler, *Managing Disagreement Constructively*, Menlo Park, California: Crisp Publishing, 1988.

Chapter 12: Inner Sources of Stress and Strength

1. S. Keen, "The Golden Mean of Roberto Assagioli," *Psychology Today*, Dec. 1974, pp. 96–107.

2. H. Stone and S. Winkelman, *Embracing Our Selves*, Los Angeles: Devorss, 1985.
Also helpful in dealing with stress of inner conflicts are R. Assagioli, *Psychosynthesis*, New York: Hobbs, Doorman, 1965;
P. Ferrucci, *What We May Be*, Los Angeles: Tarcher, 1982; and
E. O'Connor, *Our Many Selves*, New York: Harper & Row, 1971.

Chapter 13: Letting Go

1. E. R. Stauffer, *Unconditional Love and Forgiveness*, Burbank, California: Triangle, 1987.

2. Quoted in R. Fields et al, *Chop Wood, Carry Water*, Los Angeles: Tarcher, 1984.

3. A. W. Watts, *The Wisdom of Insecurity*, New York: Pantheon, 1951, p. 94.

4. R. K. Merton, "The Self-Fulfilling Prophesy," *Social Theory and Social Structure*, New York: Free Press, 1968.

5. For more information on Co-Dependence, see A. W. Schaef, *Co-Dependence*, Harper & Row, 1986. Also see M. Beattie, *Co-Dependent No More*, Hazelden, 1987.

6. S. Rinpoche, *The Tibetan Book of Living and Dying*, San Francisco: HarperCollins, 1992.

7. N. Kazantzakis, *Zorba the Greek*, New York: Touchstone, 1952.

Chapter 14: Deep Relaxation

1. H. S. Kindler, "The Influence of a Relaxation-Meditation Technique on Group Problem-Solving," *Journal of Applied Behavioral Science*, Volume 4, 1979, pp. 527–533.

2. The audiotape, "Deep Relaxation Exercises" by Dr. H. S. Kindler is available from the Center For Management Effectiveness, P.O. Box 1202, Pacific Palisades, CA 90272.

3. H. Benson, *Beyond The Relaxation Response*, New York: Berkeley Books, 1985.

Chapter 15: Reaching Out

1. J. Viorst, *Necessary Losses*, New York: Fawcett, 1986, p. 186.

Chapter 16: Honoring Your Body

1. See B. Anderson, *Stretching*, Bolinas, California: Shelter Publications, 1980; and J. Alter, *Stretch and Strengthen*, Boston: Houghton Mifflin, 1986.

2. D. Ornish, *Dr. Dean Ornish's Program For Reversing Heart Disease*, New York: Ballantine, 1990.

3. "Salt," *University of California Wellness Letter*, November, 1988.

4. B. Vitell, *A Taste of Heaven and Earth*, New York: Harper Perennial, 1993.

INDEX